FOUR WORD FILM REVIEWS

BENJ CLEWS AND MICHAEL ONESI

PRODUCERS OF WWW.FWFR.COM

AVON, MASSACHUSETTS

Published by
Adams Media, a division of F+W Media, Inc.
57 Littlefield Street, Avon, MA 02322. U.S.A.
www.adamsmedia.com

ISBN 10: 1-4405-0565-9
ISBN 13: 978-1-4405-0565-2
eISBN 10: 1-4405-0741-4
eISBN 13: 978-1-4405-0741-0

Printed in the United States of America.

10   9   8   7   6   5   4   3   2   1

Library of Congress Cataloging-in-Publication Data
is available from the publisher.

This publication is designed to provide accurate and authoritative information
with regard to the subject matter covered. It is sold with the understanding that
the publisher is not engaged in rendering legal, accounting, or other professional
advice. If legal advice or other expert assistance is required, the services of a com-
petent professional person should be sought.
—From a *Declaration of Principles* jointly adopted by a Committee of the
American Bar Association and a Committee of Publishers and Associations

Many of the designations used by manufacturers and sellers to distinguish their
product are claimed as trademarks. Where those designations appear in this book
and Adams Media was aware of a trademark claim, the designations have been
printed with initial capital letters.

This book is available at quantity discounts for bulk purchases.
For information, please call 1-800-289-0963.

Contents

Acknowledgments

We need more than four words to say thank you to all the people who helped this book get published. Thanks go out to: Courtney Miller-Callihan, who replied to our query letter seventeen minutes after we e-mailed it to her (on a Sunday night! This woman works too hard); Brendan O'Neill and the gang at Adams for their great advice and great work.

From Michael: Benj, for creating such an addictive website; Nadine Pedersen, who chatted with me for more than thirty minutes when I called her and asked, "Do you know anything about publishing? I have this idea for a book . . ."; Merilyn Simonds, who talked me off the ledge; my copyeditors (Mom, my brother Steve); my children—Katie, Olivia, and Benji—who I ignored for several months while compiling this book; the Z Boys, my lifelong friends; and finally my dad—because of your insomnia, I'm living a dream.

From Benj: Mike for saying, "This would make a great book" and then repeatedly prodding me to actually do it. I am the literary equivalent of herding cats, which makes Mike the craziest shepherd you ever heard of; my incredible wife, Lisa, for standing by me despite countless late nights in a world of my own; my brother Karl, who said "Go for it!" back when the website idea sounded insane; my dad for his long-winded jokes that showed me short is funny; and for my mum, who never got to see the first book I had published—you still inspire me.

*Four*word

An idea is like bird crap. It strikes you without warning or explanation and leaves you desperately scrabbling for paper.

In most cases, that's what all my ideas are—crappola—and if there's one thing I have got going for me, it's a big steaming pile of idea manure.

October 26, 1999, seemed like any other bad-idea day as I stared blankly at my computer screen and daydreamed about websites.

I thought of my current effort—an off-again/on-again/off-again cartoon called *technopheeb*—and about how much work it was. I thought about websites that needed no maintenance. I thought about my love of films and how cool it would be to run a film website. Then I thought about how much work it would be to write lengthy film synopses. I thought about how easy it'd be if people wrote them for me . . . and how much work it would be to read and approve all those reviews.

I went back to staring out the window as the cursor blinked back at me, judgmentally.

In that short moment of blank mindedness, almost as if to stave off the boredom, the void was suddenly filled with a dumb idea. A really dumb idea.

Perhaps a site filled with *really* short film reviews? They'd be quick and easy for people to write but, more to the point, they'd be quick and easy for me to read through.

I was surprised to find there were no other websites doing this already. (Unless you count a site that did haiku-based film reviews—

and to be honest, I wasn't even sure what haikus were, just that they were definitely longer than four words.) Suddenly my mind was buzzing with excitement for what may be the stupidest idea I'd ever had.

Not that I had the darndest inkling how long or short these reviews should be. So I set myself a challenge: write as many film reviews as I could, using the least number of words.

A frantic scribbling session followed as a flurry of short reviews came to mind. Everything from *The Godfather* to *Showgirls* (a film I hold a special place in my bowels for)—no depth was too low to be plumbed. With each effort that spilled onto the paper, I found myself chuckling more and more—this was fun!

When I was done I sat back and looked at this list—the fevered scribblings of a giggling idiot.

Some were a mammoth ten words long, too long. Then there were a few that explained themselves in six. Still too verbose for my liking. It was those reviews that summed it up in a pithy four words or less that truly caught my attention.

And so began the Four Word Film Review.

It's now been ten years that I've lived with this beast of a website. I've worked through more four word reviews than I care to remember (thankfully, a crack team of considerably smarter and more cine-literate editors came to my aid before full-blown four-word madness set in) and I've seen phenomenal talent emerge through the site in this time.

Special mention will always go to one early contributor in particular—Noncentz, a reviewer with such a rat-a-tat consistency and amazing grasp of multilayered wordplay that he set the standard for all that have followed. I have every belief he is in fact a highly advanced robotic killing machine sent from the future that somehow malfunctioned and is now writing extremely brief film reviews.

Along the way, this whole thing even made its way into newspapers and magazines around the world (*Los Angeles Times*, *New York Times*, *Chicago Sun-Times*, *Time* magazine, to name a few of the publications with *Time* in the title) and racked up a Webby Award nomination, eventually losing out to a chicken in suspenders. (Believe me, I *wish* I were making this up.)

Which brings us up to now. In a book. In your hands. In the real world.

As I write this, we're in the tenth year of the site and the breadth of films covered by more than 300,000 submitted reviews never fails to amaze me. Of course, there's absolutely no way we could ever hope to fit everything into one book (or if we did, it'd be visible from space) but I reckon we've made a pretty decent stab at it.

What lies before you is a truly unique, highly compressed look at the films you know and love or, in some cases, never heard of. (Chapter 10 is filled with reviews of silent, black-and-white films made before 1924 but don't worry if you weren't around back then— we put them all online for your viewing pleasure at *www.fourword book.com/theater*.) You will laugh, you might cry, and it could even change the way you watch films forever, as it has for many who've stumbled across the site. Just don't blame me if you find yourself visiting *www.fwfr.com* with a few reviews of your own.

—*Benj Clews (February 2010)*

In the movie *Titanic*, a large ship hits an iceberg and lots of people die. Some freeze, most drown, and one daft bugger bounces spectacularly off a propeller with a loud *tung!*

Sorry to ruin the ending but hey—we put Spoiler Alert! up there so what did you expect?

Worry not though . . . from this point on, wherever potential plot-point spoilage is looming (like a Dark Lord claiming parental rights), you'll find this little sprinkling of spoiler-warning goodness beside the movie title to keep your innocence intact.

You have been *four*warned.

The Fast and the *Four*ious

⇥ *Action* ⇤

2012 (2009)

The Day After Tomorrow director Roland Emmerich destroys the world again. The Mayans predicted the world will end in the year 2012. They were right. Starring John Cusack.

> "No Day After Tomorrow."
>
> "Cusack: John of Ark."
>
> "Please, no sea quell!"
>
> "Year, script both disastrous."

300 (2006)

In 480 BC, tens of thousands of Persian soldiers invade Greece and 300 members of the elite Spartan Guard, led by King Leonidas (Gerard Butler), put up a bloody, heroic fight.

> "Leonidas's Dismember the Titans."
>
> "Xerxes plays on 'hunch.'"
>
> "Rear penetration surprises Greeks."
>
> "Hades dining reservation announced."

Apollo 13 (1995)

Tom Hanks plays astronaut Jim Lovell in this true story about a NASA mission to the moon that goes horribly wrong. Also starring Kevin Bacon.

> "Bacon in tin can."
>
> "Lovell! Keep us together."
>
> "Ground control, Major Tom."
>
> "Hanks visits dark side."

The Bodyguard (1992)

An ex–Secret Service agent (Kevin Costner) becomes a bodyguard for a pop singer (Whitney Houston) and the pair fall in love.

> "Sexy singer uses protection."
>
> "Costner scores then shoots."
>
> "Houston sexually harasses employee."
>
> "Houston has a problem."

The Bourne Identity (2002)

Matt Damon plays Jason Bourne, a man shot and left for dead. With no memory of his past life, he discovers he has expert espionage skills. He sets out to learn about his past.

> "Matt Damon: Mini driver."
>
> "Feddies vs. Jason."
>
> "Good Will Hunted."
>
> "One Bourne, many die."

GUESS THE MOVIE

"Politician hates hot air."

Casino Royale (2006)

James Bond (Daniel Craig) earns his 00 status and goes on his first mission in this gritty film that lacks the cheesy jokes of previous 007 movies. John Cleese *does not* play M in this Bond movie.

> "Royale without Cleese."
>
> "Bond gets Foucan runaround."
>
> "Blond, James Bond."
>
> "Name's Craig. Daniel Craig."

The Da Vinci Code (2006)

Robert Langdon (Tom Hanks) is a symbologist who uncovers a centuries-old mystery involving Leonardo da Vinci, the Holy Grail, and Jesus Christ.

> "The Immaculate Deception."
>
> "Christ! Relatives!"
>
> "Hanks: You've Got Grail."
>
> "Mary marry? Quite contrary."

The Dark Knight (2008)

In this sequel to *Batman Begins*, the Caped Crusader (Christian Bale) battles the Joker, played by Heath Ledger, in one of his last roles before his untimely death.

> "An unbalanced Ledger."
>
> "The Joker Begins."
>
> "Heath Ledger's clowning glory."
>
> "Knight 'n shining harmer."

ANSWER
An Inconvenient Truth (2006)

The Day After Tomorrow (2004)

Jake Gyllenhaal and Dennis Quaid star in this environmental disaster film that features New York City being flooded and frozen over.

> "Manhattan on the rocks."
>
> "NY Sea."
>
> "NYC awash with people."
>
> "Jake Chill-enhaal."

Dirty Harry (1971)

Clint Eastwood plays cop Harry Callahan. In one scene, Harry points his gun at a robber and asks the punk if he feels lucky—did Harry fire five or six shots?

> "Punk fails elementary math."
>
> "Great cop. Bad counter."
>
> "Clint asks loaded question."
>
> "Punk receives counting lesson."

The Fast and the Furious (2001)

An undercover cop (Paul Walker) tries to infiltrate the underground world of illegal street car racing. Also starring Vin Diesel.

> "Wizard of NOS."
>
> "Walker becomes driver."
>
> "Civic disobedience."
>
> "Diesel vehicle lacks performance."

GUESS THE MOVIE "Rehash of the Titans."

Fight Club (1999)

Brad Pitt and Edward Norton play two men who start a secret, underground fight club. Also starring Meat Loaf.

> "Pits Pitt against Pitt."
>
> "Meat Loaf tenderized."
>
> "Raging (Pitt) Bull."
>
> "Two-sided love triangle."

The Fugitive (1993)

Star Wars star Harrison Ford plays Richard Kimble, a man accused of killing his wife. He goes on the run from the law (Tommy Lee Jones) to find the real murderer: the one-armed man.

> "One-armed and dangerous."
>
> "Killer leaves Ford running."
>
> "Indy and a Jones."
>
> "Killer is hand solo."

Gladiator (2000)

Maximus (Russell Crowe) is a powerful general who is betrayed by an evil prince (Joaquin Phoenix). Maximus returns to Rome as a gladiator to seek revenge. Directed by Ridley Scott.

> "Aussie and chariot."
>
> "Crowe kicks gluteus maximus."
>
> "Bird fight: Crowe, Phoenix!"
>
> "Ridleyed with Roman inaccuracies."

The Hunt for Red October (1990)

A Soviet Union captain (Sean Connery) ignores his orders and drives his submarine toward the U.S. coast. CIA agent Jack Ryan has to figure out if the rogue officer is going to attack or defect.

> "Sean of the Red."
>
> "Ryan, sea quest."
>
> "Mikhail's navy."
>
> "From Russia with Sub."

Indiana Jones and the Raiders of the Lost Ark (1981)

Whip-loving archaeologist Indiana Jones (Harrison Ford) must find the powerful Ark of the Covenant before it falls into the hands of the Nazis. (The film was released as just *Raiders of the Lost Ark* in theatres; *Indiana Jones* was added to the title for its VHS release.)

> "Jones of Ark."
>
> "Indy whips out revolver."
>
> "Arkaeologist."
>
> "Ford. Explorer."

Indiana Jones and the Temple of Doom (1984)

Indy goes to India and is asked by villagers to find a magical stone. Indy discovers a secret cult in an underground mine that has enslaved hundreds of children.

> "India 'n a Jones."
>
> "Indy's meat: the beetles."
>
> "Indy rescues Doomed kids."
>
> "Two-mb Raider."

GUESS THE MOVIE

"Alice. Tim's Wonderland."

Indiana Jones and the Last Crusade (1989)

Indy (Harrison Ford) goes on a quest to find the Holy Grail (protected by the knights of the First Crusade) with his dad (Sean Connery).

> "Drinking constitutes knight life."
> "About Last Knight."
> "Bearded Jones's Diary."
> "Seeking cup with Joneses."

Indiana Jones and the Kingdom of the Crystal Skull (2008)

An older Indy (Harrison Ford) reunites with Marion (Karen Allen) as they search for secret artifacts known as crystal skulls. This is the fourth Indiana Jones film.

> "Indy's the Marion kind?!"
> "Harrison Four-d."
> "Archaeologist seeks, becomes relic."
> "Vintage Ford still running."

Inglorious Basterds (2009)

Lt. Raine (Brad Pitt) leads a bunch of WWII Jewish-American soldiers behind enemy lines in France who terrorize, scalp, and kill Nazis. The film is directed by Quentin Tarantino.

> "Bad spellers kill Nazis."
> "Shosanna triggers Goebbel warming."
> "Reservoir Dogtags."
> "Revenge of the 'Terds."

Iron Man (2008)

Tony Stark (Robert Downey Jr.) is a CEO of a weapons-manufacturing company who designs a special metal suit that turns him into a superhero.

> "Superhero's a little rusty."
>
> "Steel from the rich."
>
> "Downey's surprisingly well cast."
>
> "'Fe' male?"

Iron Man 2 (2010)

Robert Downey Jr. returns as Tony Stark and takes on Whiplash (Mickey Rourke). Scarlett Johansson plays Black Widow.

> "Iron sequel is riveting."
>
> "Scarlett Johansson: iron maiden."
>
> "IIron Man."
>
> "Downey recast."

GUESS THE MOVIE "Spidey in arms way."

Jurassic Park (1993)

Dinosaurs are genetically re-created at an island amusement park, but when the creatures escape, island visitors run for their lives. Starring Sam Neill and Jeff Goldblum.

> "T-rex, twentieth-century toys."
>
> "Visitors feed the animals."
>
> "T-rex ignores 'Engaged' sign."
>
> "Look Back in Amber."
>
> "Neill unsurprisingly withholds endorsement."
>
> "Hammond, eggs."
>
> "T-rex isle dysfunction."
>
> "Rept-Isle."
>
> "Site for 'saur rise."
>
> "Tyrannosaurus wrecks!"
>
> "Experiment with dino sours."
>
> "Spielberg's dino-might movie."

The Lost World: Jurassic Park (1997)

Scientists return to Jurassic Park, then accidentally bring T-rexes back to San Diego. Starring Jeff Goldblum and Julianne Moore.

> "T-rex and the City."
>
> "Raiders of Lost Park."
>
> "Moore dinosaurs."
>
> "T-rex ignores immigration laws."

dinosaur © istockphoto / -ASI-

ANSWER

Spider-Man 2 (2004)

Jurassic Park III (2001)

William H. Macy and Téa Leoni play parents who trick Sam Neill into returning to the dinosaur-filled island to find their lost son.

> "Threpeatasaurus."
>
> "Dinosaurs want lunch, Téa."
>
> "Franchise close to extinction."
>
> "Third Jurrasic. Dino-snore."

Kill Bill: Vol. 1 (2003)

Uma Thurman is "The Bride," a top assassin who awakes from a coma and seeks revenge against the people who tried to kill her at her wedding. The film is directed by Quentin Tarantino.

> "Bill. Quentin. All gore."
>
> "Good Bill Hunting."
>
> "Bridesmad."
>
> "Missed honeymoon. Bride ballistic."

Kill Bill: Vol. 2 (2004)

After tracking down and killing her double-crossing assassin teammates, "The Bride" (Uma Thurman) finally confronts her ex-boss, Bill (David Carradine).

> "Second half, double Bill."
>
> "Bill killed."
>
> "Bridesmad revisited."
>
> "The No-Bill Prize."

GUESS THE MOVIE

"Documentary about roamin' emperors."

King Kong (2005)

Lord of the Rings: Return of the King director Peter Jackson remakes the 1933 classic about a giant ape that comes to New York City and falls in love with a woman (Naomi Watts).

> "Banana eater attacks Apple."
>
> "Gorilla and the Miss."
>
> "Kong avoids elevator fee."
>
> "Return of the Kong."

The Matrix (1999)

Neo (Keanu Reeves) escapes the Matrix and enters the real world where computers control humans. Is Neo the Chosen One—the only person who can save humanity?

> "Finding Neo."
>
> "Reality: bytes."
>
> "Prophet in own LAN."
>
> "Malice in Wonderland."

The Matrix Reloaded (2003)

The battle against multiple Agent Smiths to free humans from the Matrix continues in this second *Matrix* film. Neo has visions that Trinity (Carrie-Anne Moss) will be killed.

> "Keeping up with Smiths."
>
> "The One's second coming."
>
> "Alas, Smith *and* clones."
>
> "To Trinity, and beyond."

ANSWER
March of the Penguins (2005)

The Matrix Revolutions (2003)

As the machines attack Zion, Neo (who is blinded during a fight) confronts Agent Smith in the ultimate battle over the Matrix. Trinity dies trying to save Neo. Many fans and critics were disappointed with the final *Matrix* film.

> "Neo's The Zion King."
>
> "Messiah leaves holey Trinity."
>
> "Revolutions shouldn't be televised."
>
> "Neo not see."

The Messenger: The Story of Joan of Arc (1999)

Milla Jovovich plays the legendary French fighter who dies at age nineteen when she is burned at the stake by English troops in 1431.

> "Very hot story Arc."
>
> "French teen starts smoking."
>
> "Stake and French fries."
>
> "English enjoy French cooking."

Mission: Impossible (1996)

Tom Cruise plays Ethan Hunt—a secret agent accused of being a mole. To clear his name, he breaks into a secure room at CIA headquarters. Film critics complain the plot is too confusing. Also starring Jon Voight.

> "Mission impossible to understand."
>
> "Stunted actor's Impossible stunts."
>
> "Actually, mission is possible."
>
> "Voight roles in Graves."

GUESS THE MOVIE

"Watts: Tapes of Wrath."

The Mummy (1999)

Brendan Fraser and Rachel Weisz star in a new version of this classic monster tale.

> "Mummy Fear-est."
>
> "Imhotep wants his mummy."
>
> "Dumb Fraser gets Weisz."
>
> "Fraser is a raiser."

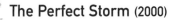

The Perfect Storm (2000)

Ocean's Eleven star George Clooney stars in this true story of the *Andrea Gail*, a deep-sea fishing boat that sank during a powerful storm in the North Atlantic Ocean in 1991.

> "Water. Ship. Drown."
>
> "Clooney's under the weather."
>
> "Gone, fishing."
>
> "Big wave goodbye."

Pirates of the Caribbean: The Curse of the Black Pearl (2003)

When Will Turner's (Orlando Bloom) girlfriend (Keira Knightley) is kidnapped by pirates, he reluctantly joins forces with Captain Jack Sparrow (Johnny Depp) to save her.

> "High-sea dead people."
>
> "Bloom has sworded affair!"
>
> "Ship of Ghouls."
>
> "Orlando thrill ride."

ANSWER

The Ring (2002)

Pirates of the Caribbean. Dead Man's Chest (2006)

Jack Sparrow (Johnny Depp) must repay his debt to Davy Jones. Also starring Orlando Bloom and Keira Knightley.

> "Sparrow becomes a swallow."
>
> "Arrr be back."
>
> "Keira: dead flat chest."
>
> "Pirates of the Carib-again."

Pirates of the Caribbean: At World's End (2007)

With Jack Sparrow (Johnny Depp) back from Davy Jones' Locker (by way of bizarre visions involving crabs and multiple Jacks), he must join forces with Captain Barbossa to journey to the world's end. Keith Richards has a cameo role as Jack's father.

> "Death. Row."
>
> "Papa's a Rolling Stone."
>
> "Johnny Depp catches crabs."
>
> "Whacked Jack brought back."

Robin Hood (2010)

Russell Crowe plays the legendary English archer in Sherwood Forest who steals from the rich to give to the poor.

> "Crowe learns arrow dynamics."
>
> "Robin is Crowe."
>
> "Early Communist redistributes wealth."
>
> "Crowe faces archery enemies."

GUESS THE MOVIE
"2 stupid 2 see."

RoboCop (1987)

When Detroit police officer Alex Murphy (Peter Weller) is fatally shot, a corporation takes the body and turns him into a robotic crime-fighter.

> "Copper is metal."
>
> "Cop literally screwed up."
>
> "Tin man gets heart."
>
> "Pig iron."

The Rock (1996)

When renegade marines take over Alcatraz, the FBI sends a weapons specialist (Nicolas Cage) and the only man to escape the supposedly inescapable prison (Sean Connery) to save the day. Also starring Ed Harris.

> "Criminal breaks into prison."
>
> "Papa, seizures, Rock."
>
> "Jail. Harris. Rock."
>
> "Scot(ch) on the Rock(s)."

Se7en (1995)

Brad Pitt and Morgan Freeman play cops investigating a series of murders that follow the seven deadly sins. The killer (Kevin Spacey) decapitates the wife (Gwyneth Paltrow) of one of the detectives.

> "Spacey planned a head."
>
> "Cop receives severance package."
>
> "Good cop, Brad cop."
>
> "Gwyneth reluctantly gives head."

Sherlock Holmes (2009)

In the Guy Ritchie version of Sherlock Holmes, the famous detective (Robert Downey Jr.) is more brawny than brainy. Jude Law plays Watson. The duo takes on Lord Blackwood (Mark Strong).

> "Holmes faces Strong adversary."
>
> "Sherlock is Guy's guy."
>
> "Law on Holmes's side."
>
> "No-shirt Sherlock."

Snakes on a Plane (2006)

Poisonous snakes are released on a plane in an attempt to kill a witness set to testify against the mob. Starring Samuel L. Jackson.

> "Boeing constrictors."
>
> "Multi-pythons, flying circuits."
>
> "Actually, snakes *in* plane."
>
> "Hijackers unarmed. (Unlegged, too.)"

Speed (1994)

Keanu Reeves plays a cop on a bus rigged with a bomb to explode if the speed drops below 50 mph. Sandra Bullock plays the unwilling bus driver and Dennis Hopper is the mad bomber.

> "Dennis Hopper's Queasy Riders."
>
> "Faster than speeding Bullock."
>
> "Unbrakeable."
>
> "Boom in public transportation."

GUESS THE MOVIE "Beware: Greeks bearing Pitts."

Spider-Man (2002)

When high-school nerd Peter Parker (Tobey Maguire) is bitten by a radioactive spider, he gains arachnid superpowers. Willem Dafoe stars as the Green Goblin, Kirsten Dunst plays Mary Jane, and James Franco is Harry Osborn.

> "Teenager wants Mary Jane."
>
> "Four Webbings and Funeral."
>
> "This Osborn is intelligible!"
>
> "Spidey cries, Uncle."
>
> "Bug hits big screen."
>
> "Teenager emits sticky substance."
>
> "Tobey joins swingers club."
>
> "Parker's web-based application."
>
> "Maguire on a wire."
>
> "Dunst tries online dating."
>
> "From acne to Arachne."
>
> "Dafoe is da foe."

Spider-Man 2 (2004)

Spider-Man (Tobey Maguire) returns to battle Dr. Octopus (Alfred Molina) while also struggling with relationship issues and failings with his superpowers.

> "Peter's temporary arachnile dysfunction."
>
> "Spidey's foe: heavily armed."
>
> "Peter can't spurt anymore."
>
> "Doc Ock rocks docks."

spider © Neubau Welt

ANSWER

Troy (2004)

Spider-Man 3 (2007)

A dark, alien substance makes Spider-Man stronger but evil. Eventually it turns photographer Eddie Brock (Topher Grace) into Venom. Thomas Haden Church plays Sandman.

> "Parker gets darker."
>
> "Dunst sings!?! D'oh, Raimi!!!"
>
> "Spidey versus quick Sand."
>
> "Vill'n Grace."

Superman (1978)

Superman (Christopher Reeve) is sent to Earth and grows up to become the Man of Steel. Gene Hackman plays villain Lex Luthor and Margot Kidder is Lois Lane.

> "Tales from the Krypt."
>
> "The Great 'S' Cape."
>
> "Reeve at breakneck speed."
>
> "L.L. Cool J(ournalist)."

SPOILER ALERT

Top Gun (1986)

Tom Cruise plays Maverick, a hotshot fighter pilot. When his wingman Goose dies, Maverick must overcome personal demons to become the best of the best. Kelly McGillis plays Cruise's love interest.

> "Goose's premature ejection fatal."
>
> "Military lowers height requirement."
>
> "Pleasure Cruise? McGillis does."
>
> "Goose should have ducked."

GUESS THE MOVIE "Cruise. Hoffman. No autism."

The Towering Inferno (1974)

A deadly fire breaks out in a newly built office tower. This disaster film features an all-star cast, including Fred Astaire.

> "Erection experiences burning sensation."
>
> "Fire with many storeys."
>
> "An Ignite to Remember."
>
> "Astaire's way to Heaven."

Troy (2004)

The Greek army, led by Achilles (Brad Pitt), goes to war against Troy, led by Prince Hector (Eric Bana). The war starts over a beautiful woman—Helen (Diane Kruger). Paris (Orlando Bloom) is easily defeated during a duel.

> "Big Fight, Greek Wedding."
>
> "Trojan horse bypasses firewall."
>
> "To Helen back."
>
> "Paris on knees, again."

Twister (1996)

A weatherman (Bill Paxton) tries to get his tornado-chasing wife (Helen Hunt) to sign divorce papers but the pair are caught up in a series of twisters.

> "Whirlwind romance."
>
> "Helen's job's a breeze."
>
> "Attack of Killer Tornadoes."
>
> "Painful dialogue breaks wind."

ANSWER

Mission: Impossible III (2006)

Under Seige (1992)

Steven Seagal plays an ex–Navy Seal, now cook, unwittingly caught aboard a terrorist-seized battleship. The film features a memorable scene where Erika Eleniak leaps topless from a cake.

> "Cake contains artificial implants."
>
> "Fry Hard."
>
> "Ship plagued by Seagal."
>
> "Seagal: Commando-n-chef."

XXX (2002)

Xander Cage (Vin Diesel) is an extreme sports athlete who the U.S. government recruits for a secret mission that takes him across a variety of continents.

> "Why? Why? Why?"
>
> "Cross continents, cross consonants."
>
> "Sequels: YYY and ZZZ."
>
> "Don't see, see, see."

GUESS THE MOVIE "Snipes on a plane."

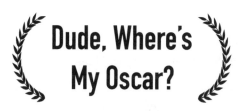

Dude, Where's My Oscar?

⤞ *Drama* ⤝

The Alamo (2004)

This film about the famous 1836 battle in Texas with Sam Houston (Dennis Quaid) and Davy Crockett (Billy Bob Thornton) was both a critical and box-office bomb.

> "Death and Texas."
>
> "Texas gets messed with."
>
> "This Alamo ironically forgettable."
>
> "Tex messaging: remember Alamo."

American Beauty (1999)

Lester (Kevin Spacey) goes through a midlife crisis by rebelling against his Realtor wife (Annette Bening), smoking drugs, and experiencing a rose-filled fantasy about his daughter's sexy high school friend.

> "Realty Bites."
>
> "Got pot. Got shot."
>
> "Dreams keep florist busy."
>
> "Guns 'n' Roses."

SPOILER ALERT

ANSWER

Passenger 57 (1992)

The Aviator (2004)

This biopic chronicles the early years of legendary businessman and aviator Howard Hughes (Leonardo DiCaprio), a man whose life was eventually ruined by his own phobias.

> "Howard's Beginning."
>
> "Hughes: The Ava Dater."
>
> "Freak went flyer."
>
> "Urine, the money."

Basic Instinct (1992)

A cop (Michael Douglas) is seduced by a beautiful novelist (Sharon Stone) who is the prime suspect of a murder case. The film is famous for the police interrogation scene where Stone uncrosses her legs to show she is wearing a miniskirt but no panties.

> "Stone's grand opening."
>
> "Police interrogate flasher."
>
> "Crossed. Un-crossed. *Hello!* Crossed."
>
> "Douglas is bed-ridden."

Boogie Nights (1997)

Mark Wahlberg plays a young man with a huge penis who becomes a famous porn star. Also starring Julianne Moore and Burt Reynolds.

> "Actor is hard-on himself."
>
> "Wahlberg's acting is stiff."
>
> "Burt's business well staffed."
>
> "Moore bangs for bucks."

GUESS THE MOVIE "Costner, Indians play charades."

The Boy in the Plastic Bubble (1976)

Saturday Night Fever star John Travolta plays Tod, a boy who is born with a weak immune system, forcing him to live his life in a sterile, plastic bubble.

> "Travolta practices safe *everything*."
>
> "Stayin' Alive in bubble."
>
> "Scientologist allergic to everything."
>
> "Tent 'n quarantino."

Braveheart (1995)

William Wallace is a Scottish commoner who leads his countrymen in a revolution for freedom from the English in Mel (*Mad Max*) Gibson's Oscar-winning historical epic.

> "Mad Macs."
>
> "Resistance is feudal."
>
> "Mel rose. Place: Scotland."
>
> "William shakes spear."

Brokeback Mountain (2005)

A story about forbidden love between two cowboys (Heath Ledger, Jake Gyllenhaal) who keep their homosexual relationship a secret for decades.

> "Irregular entry in Ledger."
>
> "Howdy life partner!"
>
> "Cowboys can't think straight."
>
> "Flaming Saddles."

ANSWER

Dances with Wolves (1990)

Cast Away (2000)

You've Got Mail star Tom Hanks plays a Federal Express executive who survives a plane crash and spends years living on an isolated, tropical island. His only companion is a volleyball named Wilson.

> "Rest of cast's away."
>
> "Wilson a beach boy."
>
> "All you've got's mail."
>
> "Hanks has a ball."

Crash (1996)

This controversial film from director David Cronenberg follows a group of people who are sexually gratified by car crashes. Starring Holly Hunter and James Spader.

> "Nude. Where's My Car?"
>
> "Auto-erotica."
>
> "Rear-ended after accident."
>
> "Sex life a wreck."

Crash (2004)

Matt Dillon plays a racist Los Angeles cop in this multi-story, Oscar-winning film that explores racism. Also starring Sandra Bullock.

> "Dillon: Ku Klux Kop."
>
> "Race, cars."
>
> "Sandra not racist? Bullocks!"
>
> "Six degrees of segregation."

GUESS THE MOVIE
"Superhero battles Venomy within."

Dances with Wolves (1990)

After an unsuccessful suicide attempt, a Civil War soldier (Kevin Costner) is sent to a frontier post where he befriends the local Sioux tribe.

> "Of bison, men."
>
> "Buffalo. Soldier."
>
> "A boy Sioux named."
>
> "From suicide to Siouxicide."

Dead Poets Society (1989)

Boarding-school students are inspired by an English professor (Robin Williams) to embrace poetry, to be free thinkers, and to seize the day. One of the students commits suicide because of an overbearing father.

> "Rhyme and Punishment."
>
> "Metaphors be with you."
>
> "Puck's performance? Mind-blowing."
>
> "Fate: verse, then death."

Driving Miss Daisy (1989)

A friendship evolves over twenty years between a bigoted Southern widow (Jessica Tandy) and her black driver (Morgan Freeman).

> "Daisy driving Morgan crazy."
>
> "Freeman's a slave driver."
>
> "Racism okay . . . she's old."
>
> "Freeman's character-driven drama."

ANSWER

Erin Brockovich (2000)

Pretty Woman star Julie Roberts plays Erin Brockovich, a law firm file clerk with a sassy attitude and big cleavage who exposes a gas company that illegally dumped toxic chemicals.

> "Gritty Woman."
>
> "Julia emphasizes two points."
>
> "She moves, mysterious waste."
>
> "Erin good at exposing."

Fahrenheit 9/11 (2004)

Documentary filmmaker Michael Moore slams President George W. Bush for his response after the terrorist attacks on September 11 and the war in Iraq.

> "Iraqnophobia."
>
> "No Moore BU**SH**."
>
> "War begins with 'W.'"
>
> "Iraqi Horror Picture Show."

Fatal Attraction (1987)

A married Michael Douglas has a one-night stand with Glenn Close. When he ends the relationship, the jilted lover terrorizes his family and boils the family's pet rabbit.

> "An affair to dismember."
>
> "Rabbit's foot not lucky."
>
> "Close reaches boiling point."
>
> "Too Close for comfort."

GUESS THE MOVIE "Robo Williams."

A Few Good Men (1992)

Two marines are charged with killing a fellow soldier. A lawyer (Tom Cruise) tries to prove Colonel Jessep (Jack Nicholson) ordered the violent hazing. The film features Nicholson's famous line "You can't handle the truth!"

> "Jack in the box."
> "Rage Against the Marine."
> "Adventures of Tom Lawyer."
> "Cruise handles truth well."

Fly Away Home (1996)

Amy (Anna Paquin) is a teenage girl who helps raise a flock of abandoned geese. She and her father (Jeff Daniels) use ultralight planes to help the geese fly south for the winter.

> "Don't go chasing waterfowls."
> "Geese is the word."
> "Delusions of gander."
> "Meet the Flockers."

Forrest Gump (1994)

Tom Hanks plays a man with a low IQ and a kind heart who becomes involved in many historical moments, including run-ins with Elvis Presley, Richard Nixon, and JFK.

> "Dense Forrest branches out."
> "Hanks for the memories."
> "Slow guy runs fast."
> "Featherbrain breezes through life."

ANSWER
Bicentennial Man (1999)

Frost/Nixon (2008)

A behind-the-scenes look at the televised interview between talk show host David Frost and disgraced U.S. president Richard Nixon regarding his involvement in the Watergate scandal.

> "Frostbitten president warms up."
>
> "Nixon taped!"
>
> "Frost nicks Dick's tricks."
>
> "Frost makes Dick shrivel."

Full Metal Jacket (1987)

Director Stanley Kubrick follows a group of marines from basic training to fighting in Vietnam. Vincent D'Onofrio plays the fat, uncoordinated recruit Gomer Pyle and Matthew Modine is Joker.

> "Art of Modine warfare."
>
> "D'Onofrio ruins clean bathroom."
>
> "Kubrick studies marine life."
>
> "Marine shoots mouth off."

Good Will Hunting (1997)

Bourne Identity star Matt Damon plays a troubled genius and Robin Williams is a washed-up therapist trying to help him. Minnie Driver stars as Damon's girlfriend.

> "Good Will toward Min."
>
> "Shrink shrinks Damon's demons."
>
> "Damon: a Bourne genius."
>
> "Math Damon."

GUESS THE MOVIE "Will Smith: Su-PR-man."

The Horse Whisperer (1998)

Robert Redford plays the horse whisperer, a trainer with the ability to understand horses. He tries to help a teen and her horse after they are involved in a horrific accident.

> "Neigh-sayer."
>
> "Redford: 'Why long face?'"
>
> "Warning: Contains foal language."
>
> "Redford learns horse code."

The Hurt Locker (2008)

Jeremy Renner plays a sergeant who takes over a bomb disposal unit in Iraq. His reckless behavior and addiction to the thrill of disarming bombs angers his fellow soldiers.

> "Comrades in disarms."
>
> "Renner's performance doesn't bomb."
>
> "Renner: war's a blast."
>
> "Soldier enjoys 'blow job.'"

Jerry Maguire (1996)

Jerry (Tom Cruise) is a sports agent who is fired from his firm. He only manages to keep one client—an arrogant football player (Cuba Gooding Jr.) who demands his agent to "show me the money!"

> "Jerry's Cuba dismissal crisis."
>
> "Afro-American demands currency display."
>
> "'Maverick' agent represents Cuba."
>
> "Hello: Renée easily had."

ANSWER

The Last Temptation of Christ (1988)

Director Martin Scorsese's controversial film portrays Jesus having sex with Mary Magdalene and the couple having a child together.

> "When Jesus came."

> "Carpenter nails Mary Magdalene."

> "Holy fuck!"

> "Crucifact and crucifiction."

Marley & Me (2008)

Newspaper columnist John (Owen Wilson) finds his dog Marley to be troublesome. But as years pass, his family grows to love the Labrador retriever. In the end, John reluctantly puts Marley down.

> "John's doggone dog gone."

> "Marley & Mediocrity."

> "Wilson files lab reports."

> "New Yeller."

Milk (2008)

Sean Penn plays Harvey Milk, one of the first openly gay politicians in the United States, who was elected to office in San Francisco. He was shot by fellow politician Dan White (Josh Brolin).

> "Crying over killed Milk."

> "Milk is o-Penn-ly gay."

> "Mourning Milk."

> "Harvey Milk encourages homogenization."

GUESS THE MOVIE "Angelina Jolie: womb radar."

Million Dollar Baby (2004)

A crusty boxing coach (Clint Eastwood) reluctantly starts training a talented female boxer (Hilary Swank).

> "Saw Swank's redemption."
>
> "Swank: belle of brawl."
>
> "Raging Belle."
>
> "Hilary, Clint on fights."

Munich (2005)

A team of Israeli secret agents hunts down and kills the people behind Black September, the terrorist group that assassinated eleven Israeli athletes and coaches at the 1972 Munich Olympics.

> "Terrorism. September. 11."
>
> "Hunt for Black September."
>
> "Meddling with Olympic terrorists."
>
> "Assassins assassinate Arab assassins."

Nixon (1995)

Oliver Stone directs this biopic of President Richard Nixon (played by Anthony Hopkins), who was forced to resign after the Watergate scandal.

> "The Unforgettable Liar."
>
> "Nix, Lies, and Audiotape."
>
> "Here lies Richard Nixon."
>
> "Welshman plays President Pinocchio."

O Brother, Where Art Thou? (2000)

George Clooney stars in this adaptation of Homer's *The Odyssey*. Three convicts in 1930s' Mississippi escape jail, record a hit song, and meet sexy sirens and a one-eyed Bible salesman.

> "Escapees leave tracks behind."
>
> "Clooney tunes."
>
> "Homer. Simpletons."
>
> "Convicts with a record."

The Passion of the Christ (2004)

Passion, directed by Mel Gibson, depicts the final hours of Jesus Christ. The crucifixion scenes of this highly profitable R-rated film are extremely gory.

> "Gory, gory, hallelujah."
>
> "Mel promotes Red Cross."
>
> "Phenomenal prophet! Phenomenal profit!"
>
> "Bruised Almighty."

The Pianist (2002)

A Jewish pianist (Adrien Brody) struggles to stay alive during the Nazi occupation of Warsaw during the Second World War.

> "Pianist's execution is off."
>
> "Invasion of Brody Snatchers."
>
> "Schindler's Lizst."
>
> "Keys to survival."

GUESS THE MOVIE   "Tom Cruise's big break."

Platoon (1986)

Oliver Stone wrote and directed this film about a young soldier (Charlie Sheen) who volunteers to serve in Vietnam and discovers the horrors of war.

> "Barnes razes village."
>
> "Charlie kills Charlie."
>
> "Charlie, Sheen."
>
> "Sheen's battle with Charlie."

Pollock (2000)

Influential artist Jackson Pollock (Ed Harris) became famous for his drip-style painting technique. Marcia Gay Harden won an Oscar for playing his wife.

> "Harris surrounded by drips."
>
> "Pollock has Gay lover."
>
> "Not typical splatter movie."
>
> "Pollock makes a splash."

Rain Man (1988)

Tom Cruise plays a hustler who goes on a cross-country road trip with his autistic half-brother Raymond (Dustin Hoffman), who turns out to be a math genius.

> "Con autist."
>
> "Isn't Cruise the idiot?"
>
> "Dustin: wizard of odds."
>
> "Raymond's pro and cons."

ANSWER
The Color of Money (1986)

Rocky (1976)

Philadelphia boxer Rocky Balboa (Sylvester Stallone) gets a once-in-a-lifetime opportunity to fight champ Apollo Creed (Carl Weathers). Talia Shire plays Rocky's love interest.

> "City of Brotherly Gloves."
> "Mumbler humbles rival rumbler."
> "Creed is good."
> "The Italian Jab."
> "Adrian: romancing the Stallone."
> "Meat tenderizer seeks opponent."
> "Shire and the ring."
> "Sly of the tiger."
> "Men fight over belt."
> "Weather(s) erodes Rock."
> "Rocky Hitting Picture Show."
> "Sly beats the meat."

Rocky Balboa (2006)

The sixth movie in this boxing franchise sees a very old Rocky (played by sixty-two-year-old Sylvester Stallone) come out of retirement to fight the reigning heavyweight champ.

> "Balboa packs a paunch."
> "The Sixth, Senseless Rocky."
> "Aging Bull."
> "Rocky's still VI-gorous."

boxing gloves © Adams Media

GUESS THE MOVIE "Jen ex."

Sarah T.—Portrait of a Teenage Alcoholic (1975)

In this TV movie, Sarah Travis (*Exorcist* star Linda Blair) is a fifteen-year-old girl who starts drinking to cope with her parent's divorce.

> "Smells like teen, spirits."
>
> "The evil in cider."
>
> "Blair repossessed by spirits."
>
> "Puberty begins with pub."

Saving Private Ryan (1998)

During the D-Day Invasion, a group of Second World War soldiers, led by Tom Hanks, must find a private (Matt Damon) whose brothers have all been killed in action.

> "Many other privates unsaved."
>
> "Tom and Jerries."
>
> "Leave? No, T.Hanks."
>
> "Brother gets own bedroom."

Schindler's List (1993)

Businessman Oskar Schindler (Liam Neeson) uses his factory as a way to save Jews from the Nazis during the Second World War.

> "Steven Spielberg's *Jews*."
>
> "Nazi tightwad saves hundreds."
>
> "Spielberg's Oskar."
>
> "Schindler pays his Jews."

Seabiscuit (2003)

Seabiscuit is an undersized horse who defies the odds to become one of the top racehorses of the Great Depression. Tobey (*Spider-Man*) Maguire plays jockey Red Pollard.

> "From nag to riches."
>
> "Little equine that could."
>
> "The Amazing Rider-Man."
>
> "Biscuit rises, wins dough."

The Shawshank Redemption (1994)

Andy Dufresne (Tim Robbins) plays an innocent accountant sent to jail for murder. He spends years in prison and befriends a fellow inmate (Morgan Freeman) before finally making his escape.

> "Accountant finds prison taxing."
>
> "Accountant of Monte Cristo."
>
> "Bible aids Andy's Exodus."
>
> "Raquel's arse hides hole."

Slumdog Millionaire (2008)

An eighteen-year-old orphan who grew up in the slums of Mumbai appears on the Indian version of *Who Wants to Be a Millionaire* in order to find the woman he loves.

> "Slum. Kind of Wonderful."
>
> "Can money Mumbai happiness?"
>
> "Beggar can be chooser."
>
> "Mumbai orphan given lifeline."

GUESS THE MOVIE "Note-worthy Holocaust survivor."

Sophie's Choice (1982)

Concentration camp survivor Sophie (Meryl Streep) is haunted by the choice Nazi guards forced her to make—pick which one of her two children lives and which one dies.

> "Meryl chooses, daughter loses."
>
> "Infant loses coin toss."
>
> "Meryl Streeped of daughter."
>
> "Poles apart."

There Will Be Blood (2007)

Daniel Plainview (Daniel Day-Lewis) plays a ruthless, turn-of-the-century oilman who will stop at nothing in his quest to become rich and powerful.

> "Oil wells, ends unwell."
>
> "Orphan. Wells."
>
> "Plainview has crude awakening."
>
> "Fuel's paradise."

They Saved Hitler's Brain (1963)

In this 1960s B movie, Nazi officials have kept Hitler's head in a jar in the hope of restoring the Third Reich. They kidnap a scientist to keep the brain alive.

> "Brine Führer."
>
> "World's least-kosher pickle."
>
> "Führer goes completely mental."
>
> "Nazis play mind games."

ANSWER

The Pianist (2002)

Titanic (1997)

Rich girl Rose DeWitt Bukater (Kate Winslet) falls in love with Jack Dawson (Leonardo DiCaprio) while on the maiden voyage of the unsinkable ship. After the boat hits an iceberg, the two scramble to stay alive.

"Sinking feelings split couple."

"Jack Dawson deflowers Rose."

"The hidden-berg disaster."

"Dumping Jack. *Splash*!"

"Girl meets buoy."

"Excess ice spoils cocktails."

"The unsinkable happens."

"Cameron's craft surprisingly see-worthy."

"A piece of ship."

"Selfish bitch hogs float."

"Problems: tip of iceberg."

"Jack D with ice."

Trainspotting (1996)

The film, starring Ewan McGregor and Robert Carlyle, follows the lives of Scottish heroin junkies.

"More like 'Veinspotting.'"

"Scottish high lads."

"Heroin, but no heroes."

"He shoots, he soars!!!"

glacier © Adams Media

GUESS THE MOVIE

"Clonin' the Barbarian."

The Truman Show (1998)

Truman (Jim Carrey) thinks he is an ordinary person until he realizes his entire life is being broadcast on television and everything around him is controlled by a TV producer.

> "True man, fake life."
>
> "To air is Truman."
>
> "The Screw Carrey Show."
>
> "Truman Shown."

Unforgiven (1992)

An aging gunslinger Bill Munny (Clint Eastwood) comes out of retirement after a bounty is put on cowboys who sliced up a prostitute. Ned (Morgan Freeman) is Munny's ex-partner.

> "Multi ho scar winner."
>
> "Frail Rider."
>
> "Munny shot."
>
> "My Munny's on Clint."

The Verdict (1982)

Paul Newman plays a hard-drinking lawyer who decides to go ahead with a medical malpractice suit instead of settling out of court and taking the easy money.

> "Newman doesn't pass bar."
>
> "Newman juggles liquor, case."
>
> "'Hello Newman.' 'Hello jury.'"
>
> "Counselor's thirst for justice."

Use the *Fours,* Luke!

⤞ *Science Fiction* ⤝

2001: A Space Odyssey (1968)

This classic film features prehistoric apes going bananas over a tall, black monolith, and HAL, a supercomputer that battles the astronauts onboard a spaceship.

> "Apes understand. I didn't."
>
> "Tall, erect column excites."
>
> "HAL controls, halts, deletes."
>
> "HAL's not user-friendly."

GUESS THE MOVIE "Least of the Mohicans."

Alien (1979)

Ellen Ripley (Sigourney Weaver) and her spaceship crewmates battle an alien that has acid for blood. The film features a memorable scene when a baby alien bursts through the chest of Kane (John Hurt).

> "The Talented Ms. Ripley."
>
> "Chest explodes. That Hurt."
>
> "Surprise guest at dinner."
>
> "Hurt can't stomach alien."
>
> "Worst indigestion ever."
>
> "Bad acid ruins trip."
>
> "Bursting with *egg*citement."
>
> "Ripley encounters Giger art."
>
> "Dinner: Hurt divides ribs."
>
> "Green Eggs and Harm."
>
> "John's inner monster exposed."
>
> "Leave ET to Weaver."

Aliens (1986)

Ellen Ripley (Sigourney Weaver) fights dozens of aliens—including the Queen alien—to save a young girl named Newt. Too bad she couldn't save Bishop (Lance Henriksen).

> "Queen attacks Ripley's Bishop."
>
> "Battle of all mothers."
>
> "Newt takes on lizard."
>
> "Queen gets sucked off."

ANSWER

Indian in the Cupboard (1995)

Alien³ (1992)

Ellen Ripley (Sigourney Weaver) shaves her head and fights more aliens. She discovers an alien egg growing inside her and kills herself to prevent the alien from being born.

> "Baldie and the Beast."
>
> "R.I.P.-ley."
>
> "Ellen Burstin'."
>
> "The Tainted Ms. Ripley."

Armageddon (1998)

A ragtag group of drillers are launched into space to destroy a large asteroid headed toward Earth. Starring Bruce Willis, Ben Affleck, and Liv Tyler.

> "Asteroid, audience bored."
>
> "World applauds exploded Bruce."
>
> "Triumph of the Drill."
>
> "Bruce has 'roid rage."

Attack of the 50 Foot Woman (1958)

Radiation from an alien encounter makes Nancy (Allison Hayes) fifty feet tall. With her new strength, she seeks revenge against her abusive husband.

> "Abused wife's anger grows."
>
> "Ascent of a Woman."
>
> "2 legs, 50 feet."
>
> "Women's cup size: ZZZZZZZZ."

GUESS THE MOVIE "Carrey: Dumb and Number."

Avatar (2009)

Paraplegic soldier Jake travels to the planet of Pandora to infiltrate the Na'vi, a race of ten-feet-tall blue people with tails, by using his avatar identity. The film is directed by James Cameron.

> "Cameron makes blue movie."
>
> "Blue man groups."
>
> "Revitalized soldier chases tail."
>
> "Army vs. Na'vi."

AVP: Alien vs. Predator (2004)

Scientists discover a pyramid buried in the Antarctic and become caught in a battle between the Aliens and the Predators.

> "Predators win cold war."
>
> "AVP: All Very Preposterous."
>
> "Predators create pyramid scheme."
>
> "Isn't Predator an alien?"

Back to the Future (1985)

Marty McFly (Michael J. Fox) travels back in time and puts his life in danger when he accidentally prevents his mom (Lea Thompson) and dad from meeting.

> "Mom doesn't recognize laundry."
>
> "20th Century Fox."
>
> "A Comedy of Eras."
>
> "Fox saved from extinction."

Blade Runner (1982)

In a futuristic world, Rick Deckard (Harrison Ford) must hunt down four illegal replicants (two of whom are played by Daryl Hannah and Rutger Hauer).

> "Repli-can't live forever."
> "Hannah and Her Resistors."
> "Han Robo."
> "Rutger's Hauers are numbered."

A Clockwork Orange (1971)

Stanley Kubrick directs this controversial film about Alex (Malcolm McDowell), a psychotic milk- and Beethoven-loving teen who undergoes experimental anti-violence therapy while in jail.

> "Delinquents go night clubbing."
> "Ludwig Van, Beat-Often."
> "Kubrick's Eyes Wide Open."
> "Lactose. Intolerance."

Close Encounters of the Third Kind (1977)

Roy (Richard Dreyfuss) has an encounter with a bright light in the sky. It leads to the discovery of a government cover-up as officials meet with aliens. The two sides use music to communicate.

> "Aliens cause mashed hysteria."
> "Martians take piano lesson."
> "Intergalactic game of Simon."
> "Space jam."

GUESS THE MOVIE
"Wray: beast supporting actress."

The Day the Earth Stood Still (1951)

An alien named Klaatu and his robot Gort land their spaceship in Washington, D.C., to deliver a very important message to the people of Earth.

> **"Pacifist alien threatens annihilation?"**
>
> **"Klaatu ignores parking regulations."**
>
> **"World According to Gort."**
>
> **"Gort: The Saucerer's Apprentice."**

District 9 (2009)

Aliens, nicknamed "Prawns," are stranded on Earth in a slum known as District 9. Sharlto Copley plays the Multi-National United official in charge of relocating the aliens to a new refugee area.

> **"Alien prawns become pawns."**
>
> **"Close encounters: third class."**
>
> **"Planned 9, outer space."**
>
> **"Illegal aliens actually aliens."**

E.T.: The Extra-Terrestrial (1982)

An alien is left behind on Earth. Three children keep him hidden from their mother and help E.T. phone home and return to his planet.

> **"Kids given the finger."**
>
> **"Alcoholic alien nearly dies."**
>
> **"Faux gnome: phone home."**
>
> **"Alien controls lunar cycle."**

ANSWER

King Kong (1933)

Face/Off (1997)

John Travolta and Nicolas Cage play mortal enemies—an FBI agent and a terrorist—who surgically swap faces.

"Facing your worst enemy."

"John dons con's face."

"Con fused with face."

"In-your-face violence."

I Am Legend (2007)

Robert Neville (Will Smith) is a scientist trying to find a cure for a plague that has left him one of the last humans on Earth.

"Will works for food."

"Sole Man."

"The Will to survive."

"The Neville Ending Story."

I, Robot (2004)

Hitch star Will Smith plays a cop investigating a murder of a scientist in the year 2035. He suspects some robots can feel emotion and are responsible for the death.

"I, bored."

"Robots with a 'Hitch.'"

"Robot goes nuts, bolts."

"Robo, cop."

GUESS THE MOVIE "The Ben Franklin Code."

Independence Day (1996)

Aliens attack Earth, destroying cities and blowing up the White House. Will Smith and Randy Quaid (playing a former alien abductee) lead the human revolt.

> "Quaid avenges anal probing."
>
> "Smith goes to Washington."
>
> "Virus crashes disks worldwide."
>
> "Aliens toast welcoming party."

Invasion of the Body Snatchers (1956)

After dozens of reports about bizarre behavior, a doctor discovers that when people fall asleep, they are being replaced by emotionless pod people.

> "Sleeping pre-seeds alien takeover."
>
> "Snatchers come in peas."
>
> "I, Pod."
>
> "Sleeping is the enemy."

Logan's Run (1976)

In the twenty-third century, survivors in a domed city are allowed to live until they are thirty and are then killed in a special ceremony. Logan's job is to kill all "runners"—people who try to escape their three-decade fate.

> "Thirty? Take up running."
>
> "'Pensioners' caught red-handed."
>
> "Life beggings at thirty."
>
> "Thirtieth birthday party ill-advised."

ANSWER

National Treasure (2004)

Men In Black (1997)

A government agency keeps track of aliens who are secretly living on Earth. Agent J (Will Smith) and Agent K (Tommy Lee Jones) play the agents in charge of protecting our planet.

> "J, K prowling."
>
> "Alien, Smith, and Jones."
>
> "Jones flashes Smith repeatedly."
>
> "Mexican actually illegal alien."

Planet of the Apes (1968)

Astronauts crash on a planet where apes rule and humans are slaves. The film features a famous scene involving the Statue of Liberty. Starring Charlton Heston.

> "Astronauts discover Banana Republic."
>
> "Enslaved Heston finds Liberty."
>
> "Luckily, monkeys speak English."
>
> "Apes revolutionize gorilla warfare."

Predator (1987)

While on a mission in the jungle, a group of commandos (led by actors-turned-governors Arnold Schwarzenegger and Jesse Ventura) are stalked and killed by an alien hunter.

> "Arnie butchers alien/English."
>
> "Austrian Oak in woods."
>
> "Jesse Ventura: E.T. Detective."
>
> "Governors fight illegal alien."

GUESS THE MOVIE "Stone: grassy know-all."

Soylent Green (1973)

Charlton Heston plays a detective living in a futuristic, overpopulated world where food is scarce. He discovers the shocking secret behind Soylent Green ration wafers—they're made of people.

> "Heston eats baked beings."

> "Man, what's eating Heston?"

> "Fed up with people."

> "Heston realizes everyone's crackers."

Star Trek: The Motion Picture (1979)

The classic sci-fi TV series debuts on the big screen in a film that critics complain is too slow and boring. Starring William Shatner and Leonard Nimoy.

> "Trek: The Motionless Picture."

> "Chrome dome hones drone."

> "Jim, beam."

> "Banal. Probe."

Star Trek III: The Search for Spock (1984)

The crew of the Enterprise go in search of Spock following his apparent death in *Star Trek II*.

> "Spocktacular rebirth."

> "Live again and prosper."

> "Kirk depressed. Bones possessed."

> "Finding Nimoy."

ANSWER

JFK (1991)

Star Trek: Generations (1994)

Two *Star Trek* captains (William Shatner, Patrick Stewart) join forces to stop an intergalactic madman.

> "Battle of done Kirk."
>
> "Kirk visits final frontier."
>
> "You're dead, Jim."
>
> "Kirk becomes Bones."

Star Trek: Nemesis (2002)

This *Star Trek* film features a cloned version of Captain Picard and a twin of the android Data.

> "E.T. foe: clone."
>
> "Control, alter-ego, delete."
>
> "Hoist by own Picard."
>
> "Back up your Data."

Star Trek

2009

The story of how the Enterprise crew first met at Starfleet Academy. James Kirk (Chris Pine) is a reckless troublemaker while Spock (Zachary Quinto) is romantically involved with Uhura (Zoe Saldana).

> "Star Trek: First Generation."
>
> "Uhura makes Spock pointy."
>
> "Young Kirk's a jerk."
>
> "Start Trek."

GUESS THE MOVIE "Naomi becomes Kong-cubine."

Star Wars: Episode I—The Phantom Menace (1999)

Two Jedi knights rescue Queen Amidala (Natalie Portman), then crash-land on a planet where they meet young Anakin Skywalker (Jake Lloyd)—the boy who will one day become Darth Vader.

> "Poor little orphan Ani."
>
> "Sith hits the fans."
>
> "Anakid."
>
> "Jedi chopping Maul."

Star Wars: Episode II—Attack of the Clones (2002)

Anakin (Hayden Christensen) and Amidala (Natalie Portman) begin to fall in love in this film that features an ass-kicking fight scene with Yoda. Starring Ewan McGregor.

> "Amputation runs in family."
>
> "Clones are Jango counterFetts."
>
> "The Emperor's new clones."
>
> "Ewan, who's army?"

Star Wars: Episode III—Revenge of the Sith (2005)

Anakin is tricked into joining the Dark Side. After a fight with Obi-Wan Kenobi leaves him physically scarred, Anakin dons the famous black uniform of Darth Vader.

> "Anakin: 'I'll be black.'"
>
> "Mr. and Mrs. Sith."
>
> "Lucas makes ends meet."
>
> "Turn of the Jedi."

ANSWER

Star Wars: Episode IV—A New Hope (1977)

A simple farm boy named Luke Skywalker (Mark Hamill) teams up with Han Solo (Harrison Ford), Obi-Wan Kenobi (Alec Guinness), C3PO, and R2D2 to battle Darth Vader and save rebel leader Princess Leia (Carrie Fisher).

"Vader downs a Guinness."

"Pilot tested for 'steroids."

"Luke likes kissing sister."

"Sore throat rules space."

"Sand, Ford and son."

"In death, Obi won."

"Luke: next of 'Kin."

"Hamill and cheese."

"Career in agriculture abandoned."

"Fourth Be With You."

"Poofy android befriends mailbox."

"Original space 'n' Vader."

Star Wars: Episode V—The Empire Strikes Back (1980)

Luke meets Yoda in the swamps of Dagobah to begin his Jedi training. Later, he loses his arm during a fight with Darth Vader before learning that Vader is his father.

"Luke swamped with schoolwork."

"Tool Hand Luke."

"Luke. Pa. No hand."

"Surprising foe pa."

GUESS THE MOVIE

"Tobey Maguire: Amazing Ciderman."

Star Wars: Episode VI—Return of the Jedi (1983)

Han Solo is rescued from Jabba the Hutt. With the help of the Ewoks, Luke Skywalker, and friends, the Rebel Alliance successfully defeats Darth Vader and the Empire.

> "Slug, Fisher into bondage."
>
> "Father taken off respirator."
>
> "Han's free."
>
> "Bears host Skywalker roast."

Starship Troopers (1997)

Young soldiers (led by *Doogie Howser* star Neil Patrick Harris) battle alien insects.

> "The War on Bugs."
>
> "Bug really kills, 90210."
>
> "Doogie Howitzer."
>
> "Interstellar insecticide."

The Terminator (1984)

A cyborg (Arnold Schwarzenegger) travels back in time to murder the mother of a future rebel leader. Michael Biehn plays the soldier sent to protect her.

> "Arnold practices *extreme* contraception."
>
> "Governor Arnold's first 'Term.'"
>
> "Human Biehn versus cyborg."
>
> "Die Robot."

ANSWER

The Cider House Rules (1999)

Terminator 2: Judgment Day (1991)

Arnold Schwarzenegger plays a cyborg sent to protect John Connor from a shape-shifting terminator (Robert Patrick) made of liquid metal.

"Arnie vs. thermometer contents."

"I'm smelllllting! Smelllllting!!!"

"Old red eyes back."

"Arnold becomes sur-robot father."

Terminator 3: Rise of the Machines (2003)

John Connor (Nick Stahl), future leader of the human resistance against the machines, is hunted by a female terminator. Arnold Schwarzenegger plays Connor's robotic protector.

"The Terminat*her*."

"Arnie's femme metale."

"Terminator terminated terminating terminatress."

"III, Robot."

Terminator Salvation (2009)

The machines have taken over and John Connor (Christian Bale) must organize and lead the human survivors in order to save humanity.

"IV'll be back."

"Christian plays J.C."

"Connor's rage against machines."

"Christian promises Salvation."

GUESS THE MOVIE
"Wallace: tortured and kilt."

Total Recall (1990)

Arnold Schwarzenegger plays a man whose memories have been tampered with. He must head to Mars to find out his true identity.

> "Martians fidget with midget."
>
> "Strife on Mars."
>
> "Ungovernable freaks support Schwarzenegger."
>
> "Schwarzenegger's 'Recall' campaign succeeds."

Transformers (2007)

A teenager (Shia LaBeouf) buys his first car, which turns out to be an alien robot named Bumblebee. They become involved in a battle between the Autobots and the Decepticons.

> "More than meets CGI."
>
> "Metamotorphosis."
>
> "Humans fight with traffic."
>
> "Transforms $9 into disappointment."

Transformers: Revenge of the Fallen (2009)

Director Michael Bay, along with stars Shia LaBeouf and Megan Fox, return for another battle between the Autobots and the Decepticons.

> "Mechanomorphism's second grind around."
>
> "Mega Fox."
>
> "T2: Judgment Bay."
>
> "TransforMores."

War of the Worlds (2005)

Tom Cruise must protect his family as aliens attack Earth. The evil E.T.'s are eventually stopped because they have no immunity to human viruses.

"Aliens paint town red."

"Cruise Encounters Third Kind."

"Aliens? Send Cruise, missiles."

"Flew in; flu, out."

GUESS THE MOVIE "Sci-fi HAL of fame."

Show Me the Funny

→ Comedy ←

The 40-Year-Old Virgin (2005)

When Andy's (Steve Carell) coworkers learn he has never had sex, they make it their mission to help him lose his virginity.

> "Long time no she."
>
> "Salesman finally achieves penetration."
>
> "Celibate good times, c'mon!"
>
> "Carell explores virgin territory."

50 First Dates (2004)

Henry (Adam Sandler) befriends Lucy (Drew Barrymore) on a chance meeting. His plans to woo her are complicated when he discovers she suffers from daily memory loss.

> "Sandler's kiss, apparently forgettable."
>
> "Drew forgets. Audience envious."
>
> "Drew a blank."
>
> "Groundhog Dates."

American Pie (1999)

This comedy about horny teens is famous for a scene involving Jason Biggs having sex with an apple pie.

> "Jim's a piesexual."
> "Pie Who Shagged Me."
> "Apple pie loses cherry."
> "Passion of the Crust."

Anger Management (2003)

Dave Buznik (Adam Sandler) is ordered by a judge to take anger management courses from unconventional therapist Dr. Buddy Rydell (Jack Nicholson).

> "Book Jack in anger."
> "Unhappy Gilmore."
> "Mad in Manhattan."
> "Audience should be furious."

Animal House (1978)

This college comedy starring John Belushi focuses on frat-house fun at Delta House. It is one of actor Kevin Bacon's first movies.

> "From Beer to Fraternity."
> "Kevin Bacon's first degree."
> "Frat's entertainment!"
> "American Phi."

GUESS THE MOVIE "Morgan Freemandela."

Austin Powers: International Man of Mystery (1997)

A 1960s shag-loving, psychedelic British spy (Mike Myers) lands in the 1990s to try to stop Dr. Evil in this spoof of James Bond movies.

> "Gr007y."
>
> "Double Oh Behave!"
>
> "Spy lacks dental plan."
>
> "Austin triumphs over Evil."

Austin Powers: The Spy Who Shagged Me (1999)

Austin (Mike Myers) must battle Fat Bastard, Mini-Me, Dr. Evil, and Scott Evil to retrieve his mojo.

> "Americans now understand 'shagged.'"
>
> "Scott Evil, evil Scot."
>
> "Shag to the Future."
>
> "Attack of the mini-clone."

Austin Powers in Goldmember (2002)

Austin Powers travels to 1975 and hooks up with Foxy Cleopatra (Beyoncé) and his dad (Michael Caine) in order to stop the Dutch madman Goldmember.

> "To insanity and Beyoncé!"
>
> "Beyoncéing back to 1975."
>
> "Father, son, wholly gauche."
>
> "Please say never again."

Babe (1995)

In this heartwarming family film, Babe is a young pig living on a farm who dreams of becoming a sheepdog. Farmer Hoggett eventually enters Babe in a sheepdog-herding contest.

"Ham actor wins prize."

"Look, Ewes Talking!"

"Breakfast meat unclogs hearts."

"Fairgoers enjoy pig's feat."

Best in Show (2000)

From the team that brought you *This Is Spinal Tap*, this comedy mocks dog shows and crazy canine owners.

"Dogs inspire biting humor."

"Sit happens."

"Dog beat dog world."

"This Is Spaniel Tap."

Blades of Glory (2007)

Two brawling, figure skating rivals (Jon Heder and *Talladega Nights* star Will Ferrell) are kicked out of the sport. They discover a loophole and return as the sport's first male pairs skating team.

"Ice guys finish first."

"Will, but no grace."

"Two putzes, triple lutzes."

"Talladega Tights."

GUESS THE MOVIE "Run from Forest, run!"

The Blues Brothers (1980)

Newly released from prison, Jake and Elwood Blues (John Belushi, Dan Aykroyd) try to get their old band together for a fundraising concert to save an orphanage.

> "Robber band."
>
> "Band on the run."
>
> "Reformed felon reforms band."
>
> "Band of Brothers."

Borat: Cultural Learnings of America for Make Benefit Glorious Nation of Kazakhstan (2006)

Sacha Baron Cohen plays a reporter from Kazakhstan who travels across the United States to discover America and take Pamela Anderson as his wife by putting her in a traditional Kazakhstan marriage sack.

> "Borat misunderkazakhstanding."
>
> "Ela*borat*e prankster."
>
> "Anderson: hopeless in sack."
>
> "Make benefit Cohen's wallet."

Bull Durham (1988)

Crash Davis (Kevin Costner) and Nuke LaLoosh (Tim Robbins) are minor-league baseball players both chasing after the same groupie (Susan Sarandon).

> "Players desperately seeking Susan."
>
> "Baseball diamond. Love triangle."
>
> "Batsman and Robbins."
>
> "Field of Wet Dreams."

ANSWER

Last King of Scotland (2006)

Caddyshack (1980)

Bill Murray and Chevy Chase star in an *Animal House*–style comedy about a posh country club. Rodney Dangerfield plays an obnoxious golfer who clashes with club officials.

> "Dangerfield's golf war syndrome."
>
> "Golf coarse."
>
> "Humor is above par."
>
> "Dangerfield drinks, drives."

Calendar Girls (2003)

In this British film, a group of middle-aged women decide to pose nude for a calendar to raise money for leukemia research. Starring Helen Mirren and Julie Walters.

> "Twelve months of wither."
>
> "Is Saguary a month?"
>
> "Centerolds."
>
> "Those '70s show."

Chasing Amy (1997)

Ben Affleck plays a comic book artist who falls in love with a graphic novelist (Joey Lauren Adams), despite the fact that she is a lesbian. Kevin Smith writes and directs.

> "Apparently sexuality's a phase."
>
> "Graphic novelist's relationship sketchy."
>
> "Affleck makes Les miserable."
>
> "Chasing Sexual Identity."

GUESS THE MOVIE "Halle makes cat shit."

Clerks (1994)

Dante Hicks is an unmotivated convenience store worker who spends a day at work talking with friends and dealing with weird customers.

> "Both clerks are jerks."
>
> "American idles."
>
> "Dante's divine comedy."
>
> "Dante's antics counter productive."

Coyote Ugly (2000)

An aspiring songwriter moves to New York City and gets a job in a wild bar filled with hot, sexy bartenders.

> "Bar belles."
>
> "Hottest girls bar none!"
>
> "Lady bartenders call shots."
>
> "Tap dancers."

The Devil Wears Prada (2006)

Anne Hathaway plays a young, naive woman who gets a job at a major fashion magazine working for cold and ruthless editor Miranda Priestly (Meryl Streep).

> "Satin worship."
>
> "Fear and clothing."
>
> "Wolf in Streep's clothing."
>
> "Fashist leader."

ANSWER

Catwoman (2004)

Dr. Strangelove or: How I Learned to Stop Worrying and Love the Bomb (1964)

U.S. officials try to stop an atomic bomb that is headed toward the USSR. This Stanley Kubrick-directed film features Peter Sellers and Slim Pickens.

> "Classic Kubrick. Best Sellers."
>
> "Strangelove lacks 'arm' control."
>
> "World's survival chance: Slim."
>
> "The Kubrick Missile Crisis."

Dumb & Dumber (1994)

Jim Carrey and Jeff Daniels play moronic friends who go on a cross-country trip to return a suitcase full of cash to its beautiful owner.

> "Gets worse and worser."
>
> "Two guys, zero brains."
>
> "Dumb: Kind of Wonderful."
>
> "Simple Twits of Fate."

Good Morning Vietnam (1987)

Robin Williams plays a U.S. military radio DJ during the Vietnam War who is popular with soldiers, but his unconventional humor angers army brass.

> "CO KOs GI DJ."
>
> "'Nam radio ham."
>
> "DJ Williams is Hanoi-ing."
>
> "Saigon the air."

GUESS THE MOVIE "Talking finger has laryngitis."

Groundhog Day (1993)

Bill Murray stars as a weatherman stuck in a time warp. He keeps reliving the same twenty-four hours over and over—Groundhog Day in Punxsutawney, Pennsylvania.

> "Daily events repeat themselves."
>
> "Daily events repeat themselves."
>
> "Daily events repeat themselves."
>
> "Daily events repeat themselves."

The Hangover

2009

Four friends head to Las Vegas for a bachelor party and wake up the next morning with the groom missing and no memory of what happened the night before.

> "What happened in Vegas?"
>
> "Memory loss Vegas."
>
> "Forgotten night. Unforgettable comedy."
>
> "Three Drunks and Baby."
>
> "Heaving Las Vegas."
>
> "Total Non-Recall."
>
> "Floored groomsmen. Roof-ed groom."
>
> "Beer, loathing, Las Vegas."
>
> "Tyson pissed? Easy Tiger!"
>
> "What tigers dream of."
>
> "Stags rampage through Vegas."
>
> "Tased and Confused."

ANSWER

The Shining (1980)

Harold & Kumar Go to White Castle (2004)

John Cho and Kal Penn play stoners on a quest—they spend the night searching for White Castle hamburgers to satisfy their munchies.

> "W.C. field trip."
> "Friends seek holy grill."
> "Starving stoners shatter stereotypes."
> "Rage Against the Munchies."

Harvey (1950)

Jimmy Stewart plays a lovable drunk who is due to be committed to a mental institution after befriending Harvey, a six-foot rabbit nobody else can see.

> "Psychiatrists go rabbit hunting."
> "Story of rabbitual drinker."
> "Show me the bunny."
> "Stewart energized by bunny."

Home Alone (1990)

A large family leaves for vacation and forgets to bring eight-year-old Kevin (Macaulay Culkin). Now he must protect his house from two bungling criminals (Joe Pesci, Daniel Stern).

> "I'd abandon Culkin, too."
> "Pesky kid defeats Pesci."
> "Documentary to promote abortion."
> "Culkin toys with burglars."

GUESS THE MOVIE

"Documentary. Eco logic AI."

Honey, I Shrunk the Kids (1989)

Rick Moranis plays a scientist who invents a shrinking machine that accidentally zaps his children and their friends.

> "Inventor experiences little success."
> "Kids are a handful."
> "Poor little Rick's girl."
> "Wee Are the Children."

Junior (1994)

In this pregnant man comedy, *The Terminator* star Arnold Schwarzenegger plays a fertility research scientist who agrees to carry an embryo in his body.

> "Governor goes full term."
> "Girly man."
> "Make womb for daddy."
> "Arnie doesn't terminate."

Knocked Up (2007)

Career-minded E! network broadcaster Alison (Katherine Heigl) becomes pregnant after a one-night stand with a lazy slacker (Seth Rogen). The strangers get to know each other as they prepare for the baby's arrival.

> "E! girl gets F'd."
> "Lazy bastard fathers bastard."
> "Unemployed Rogen's labor problem."
> "Heigl's crowning achievement."

Liar Liar (1997)

A son's birthday wish comes true—for one day, his lawyer father (Jim Carrey, star of *The Truman Show*) is unable to tell a lie.

"The 'Truth Man' Show."

"Carrey: The Lyin' King."

"Carrey suffers truth ache."

"Carrey represents without misrepresentation."

Mamma Mia! (2008)

Sophie invites three men to her wedding, hoping to figure out which one is her dad, despite her mom's (Meryl Streep) wishes. This musical is based on the hit songs of Swedish band ABBA.

"Fathers: more the Merylier."

"Streep throat proves infectious."

"Meryl's daughter Bjorn illegitimate."

"Three men and ABBAby."

Monty Python and the Holy Grail (1975)

John Cleese and the rest of the Python comedy troupe put their humorous spin on the King Arthur legend. Arthur's limb-chopping fight with the Black Knight is hilarious.

"Royale with Cleese."

"Knight: disarmed and dangerous."

"Ni-slapper."

"Farewell to arms, legs."

GUESS THE MOVIE "Ballet Elliot."

Mrs. Doubtfire (1993)

A divorced actor (*Mork & Mindy* star Robin Williams) disguises himself as an old woman and takes a job as his ex-wife's nanny so he can spend more time with his children.

> "Williams plays 'Tootsie' role."
>
> "Funny tranny granny nanny."
>
> "Williams—Mork or Mindy?"
>
> "Mork, with norks."

Multiplicity (1996)

An overworked construction worker (Michael Keaton)—too busy to keep up his family commitments—clones himself.

> "Keaton is clone arranger."
>
> "Michael Keaton's beside himself."
>
> "Three Keatons too many."
>
> "Keaton multiplies, goes fourth."

My Best Friend's Wedding (1997)

Julianne (Julia Roberts) realizes she is in love with her best friend (Dermot Mulroney) when he announces he's getting married (to Cameron Diaz). Roberts tries to break up the happy couple.

> "My Best Friend's Meddling."
>
> "Bridesmaid wants a promotion."
>
> "Women pursue One Ring."
>
> "Diaz adorable, Roberts deplorable."

ANSWER
Billy Elliot (2000)

My Big Fat Greek Wedding (2002)

The daughter of Greek immigrants (Nia Vardalos) falls in love and gets engaged to a non-Greek man (John Corbett)—to the dismay of her traditional family.

"For feta or worse."

"Grecian formulaic comedy."

"Funny as Hellenism."

"Beware: Greeks, wedding gifts."

Napoleon Dynamite (2004)

Napoleon Dynamite is a nerdy teenager with very poor dance skills who helps his friend Pedro run for high school president.

"Dancing 'n' the Dork."

"Politically motivated square dancing."

"Napoleon in social exile."

"Crouching Liger, Hideous Dancing."

Pineapple Express (2008)

Marijuana enthusiast Dale (Seth Rogen) witnesses a crooked cop kill a drug lord and goes on the run with his dealer Saul (James Franco). The film climaxes with a shootout.

"Rogen's high-concept thriller."

"Franco, Rogen's joint venture."

"Franco, Rogen: best buds."

"Dale smokes killers."

GUESS THE MOVIE "Two balls? You're out!"

Pretty Woman (1990)

A businessman (Richard Gere) breaks up with his girlfriend, then hires a prostitute (Julia Roberts) for a week to attend social functions with him.

> "Gere is buy-sexual."
>
> "Whore explores stores galore!"
>
> "Whore-to-culture exhibition."
>
> "Shags to riches."

Risky Business (1983)

With his parents away on vacation, Joel (Tom Cruise) makes money to pay for the Porsche he accidentally trashed by running a brothel out of his home with the help of a sexy hooker (Rebecca De Mornay).

> "Show me De Mornay!"
>
> "Skivvied Scientologist sings Seger."
>
> "Cruise left 'Ho alone."
>
> "Cruise plays pimp-ly teen."

Runaway Bride (1999)

Pretty Woman star Julia Roberts plays a woman who has a habit of running away from her fiancés at the altar.

> "Julia's altar ego."
>
> "Pretty Fast Woman."
>
> "The Wedding Dasher."
>
> "Julia has prior engagements."

ANSWER
A League of Their Own (1992)

School of Rock (2003)

A broke rocker (Jack Black) lies his way into a job as a substitute teacher at a private school, then decides to enter his young students into a battle of the bands contest.

> "Jack the Riffer."
> "Rock. Enroll!"
> "Wee Will Rock You."
> "Schoolhouse Rock."

The Seven Year Itch (1955)

This film is best known for its famous scene of Marilyn Monroe standing on a sidewalk subway grate as the wind blows her white skirt.

> "Gown with the Wind."
> "Devil in blew dress."
> "Marilyn Monroe's grate performance."
> "Marilyn gets blown up."

Sex and the City: The Movie (2008)

Carrie and Big decide to get married and her friends—Samantha, Charlotte, and Miranda—are thrilled. But during the rehearsal dinner, a comment from Miranda accidentally gives Big cold feet.

> "Wedding's getting Carrie'd away."
> "Carrie marries? Big deal!"
> "Big fat Big wedding."
> "Miranda, Steve bridge differences."

GUESS THE MOVIE "To Serve with Love."

Superbad (2007)

Foul-mouthed high school buddies (Michael Cera, Jonah Hill) spend the night trying to find booze for a party. Best part of the movie—Fogell and his McLovin fake ID.

> "Cruisin' for a boozin'."
>
> "I McLoved it."
>
> "Not super, not bad."
>
> "Boys development, almost arrested."

There's Something About Mary (1998)

Ted (Ben Stiller) hires a private eye to find his old high-school prom date, Mary (Cameron Diaz). The film features a memorable scene involving semen and Mary's hair.

> "Emergency room nut case."
>
> "Cameron's hair-raising experience."
>
> "There's Semen About Mary."
>
> "Boy with pearl earring."

This Is Spinal Tap (1984)

Christopher Guest's mock documentary about a washed-up rock band touring across the United States.

> "Two words: shit sandwich."
>
> "Sex, drugs, mock, roll."
>
> "11 out of 10."
>
> "Guest guitarist."
>
> "Drummers constantly spontaneously combusting."
>
> "Dwarf almost tramples Stonehenge."
>
> "Cucumber triggers security scare."
>
> "Dumb and drummers."
>
> "Derek Smalls' big cucumber."
>
> "Hugeness of Stonehenge understated."
>
> "Help wanted: inflammable drummer."
>
> "The mocksters of rock."

Tootsie (1982)

A struggling actor (Dustin Hoffman) pretends to be a woman and lands a role on a soap opera.

> "Hoff-man, Hoff-woman."
>
> "That Dorothy has balls . . ."
>
> "Hoffman overdoes dress rehearsal."
>
> "Dustin skirts the issue."

guitar © Neubau Welt

GUESS THE MOVIE "Cusack to the Future."

Tropic Thunder (2008)

Spoiled actors filming a Vietnam War movie become involved in a real war with drug dealers. Robert Downey Jr. plays an actor who dyes his skin to portray an African-American soldier.

> "Robert Browney Jr."
>
> "Downey joins dark side."
>
> "(If) We Were Soldiers."
>
> "Platoon lampoon."

Wedding Crashers (2005)

Swingers star Vince Vaughn and Owen Wilson play buddies who crash wedding parties to drink free booze and pick up bridesmaids.

> "Vaughn: The Wedding Swinger."
>
> "Bridesmaids are visited."
>
> "Sex after marriage."
>
> "Always (with) a bridesmaid."

Yes Man (2008)

Carl (*The Cable Guy* star Jim Carrey) takes a self-help course that encourages him to change his attitude by saying yes to everything.

> "Carrey, the concurring hero."
>
> "Jim Carrey: Able Guy."
>
> "Excess stress on yes."
>
> "Carrey endorses affirmative action."

Young Frankenstein (1974)

Mel Brooks puts his comedic spin on the classic monster tale.
The film stars Gene Wilder (Dr. Frankenstein), Gene Hackman
(Blindman), and Peter Boyle (the Monster).

"Frankenstein's Wilder days."

"Wilder joins corpse pieces."

"Wilder develops monstrous Boyle."

"Monster's pair of Genes."

GUESS THE MOVIE "Cowboys ride each other."

Keanu Wins Acting Oscar

↣ *Fantasy* ↢

Barbarella (1968)

In the year 40,000, Barbarella (Jane Fonda) is an astronaut from Earth who goes on various sexual adventures in outer space.

> "I'm Fonda title sequence."
>
> "A Dish Called Fonda."
>
> "Astronaughty."
>
> "Lust in Space."

Big (1988)

A young boy wishes he was big. When he wakes the next morning, he is an adult. Starring Tom Hanks (*Toy Story*).

> "Kid-life crisis."
>
> "Tom Hanks: Boy Story."
>
> "Tomboy."
>
> "Hanks grows—big pianist."

Catwoman (2004)

Halle Berry in a sexy leather outfit is the only good thing in this movie that many critics called the worst film of the year. Also starring Sharon Stone (*Basic Instinct*).

> "Sharon Stone . . . pussy . . . familiar?"
>
> "Not up to scratch."
>
> "Feline hot, hot, hot!"
>
> "*Purr*suit of Crappyness."

Charlie and the Chocolate Factory (2005)

Five children win a once-in-a-lifetime prize—a tour of the magical chocolate factory run by Willy Wonka (Johnny Depp).

> "Bonbon voyage."
>
> "Families enjoy Depp's Willy."
>
> "Depped in chocolate."
>
> "Industry turns river brown."

The Chronicles of Narnia: The Lion, the Witch and the Wardrobe (2005)

Four children discover a magical wardrobe that leads them to Narnia, a special world where animals (including beavers) talk. Tilda Swinton plays the evil White Witch and Liam Neeson voices Aslan the lion.

> "White Witch real bitch."
>
> "Lion Neeson."
>
> "Teen boys chase beaver."
>
> "Wardrobe malfunction precipitates exposure."

GUESS THE MOVIE "Ryan's privates saved."

Conan the Barbarian (1982)

When his village is attacked and his parents are killed, a young Conan is enslaved. When he grows up and becomes a mighty warrior, he seeks revenge. Starring Arnold Schwarzenegger.

> "Austrian Oak: wooden swordsman."
>
> "Schwarzenegger. Swords 'n' anger."
>
> "That's *Governor* the Barbarian."
>
> "Arnold kicks asp."

The Crow (1994)

A year after Eric (Brandon Lee) and his girlfriend were murdered, Eric comes back to life and seeks vengeance. Lee was accidentally shot and killed during the filming of this movie.

> "Silent but dead Lee."
>
> "As the crow dies."
>
> "Crow is raven mad."
>
> "Brandon: extreme method actor."

The Curious Case of Benjamin Button (2008)

Brad Pitt plays Benjamin Button, a person who was born an old man and then ages backwards.

> ".sega ttiP"
>
> "Pitt turns life around."
>
> "The Born Old Entity."
>
> "Coming of youth story."

Edward Scissorhands (1990)

Johnny Depp plays a quiet man with scissors for hands who lives alone in a mansion. A kind woman discovers him and invites him into her home. Also starring Winona Ryder and Vincent Price.

> "Price dies beforehand."
>
> "Sheeeeears Johnny!"
>
> "How does Depp wipe?"
>
> "Depp's heavy-handed comedy."

Eternal Sunshine of the Spotless Mind (2004)

When a couple's romance (*Ace Ventura: Pet Detective* star Jim Carrey, and Kate Winslet) goes bad, they undergo a procedure to erase memories of the relationship from their minds.

> "Carrey's erase against time."
>
> "Boy m_ets g___."
>
> "Erase Ventura: Past Defective."
>
> "An Affair to Forget."

Excalibur (1981)

The story of King Arthur and the Knights of the Round Table and the forbidden love between Guinevere and Sir Lancelot. Arthur pulls the magical sword Excalibur from a stone to become king.

> "Watery tart dispenses sword."
>
> "Lancelot without pantsalot."
>
> "Death of a Grailsman."
>
> "Excalibore."

GUESS THE MOVIE "Hanks experiences crash diet."

Field of Dreams (1989)

A mysterious voice convinces Ray (Kevin Costner) that if he builds a baseball diamond on his Iowa cornfield, legendary player Shoeless Joe Jackson will come.

> "Everybody loves Ray's mound."
>
> "Corn farmer unearths diamond."
>
> "Farm team crops up."
>
> "Iowa mistaken for Heaven."

Ghost (1990)

After being murdered, Sam (Patrick Swayze) uses a psychic (Whoopi Goldberg) to help warn and protect his wife (Demi Moore). The film features a famous pottery love scene.

> "Whoopi cushions Demi's grief."
>
> "Horny Potter."
>
> "Goldberg's medium: well done."
>
> "Swayze's into making Whoopi."

Ghost Rider (2007)

Johnny Blaze (Nicolas Cage) is Ghost Rider, a supernatural bounty hunter whose skull and motorcycle are covered in flames.

> "Cage drives a Blazer."
>
> "Hot wheels."
>
> "Cage's vicious cycle."
>
> "Cage has Hell toupee."

ANSWER
Cast Away (2000)

Harry Potter and the Sorcerer's Stone (2001)

In the first film based on J. K. Rowling's book series, Harry (Daniel Radcliffe) discovers he is the son of famous wizards and begins his schooling at Hogwarts School of Witchcraft. The film is directed by Chris Columbus.

> "Columbus discovers magical land."
>
> "Son of a witch."
>
> "School for wiz kids."
>
> "School teacher turns tricks."

Harry Potter and the Chamber of Secrets (2002)

Harry ignores Dobby's warnings of mortal danger and returns to Hogwarts. A monster escapes from the Chamber of Secrets and stalks the students.

> "Dobby: Gollum with manners."
>
> "Welcome back, Potter."
>
> "Harry speaks: forked tongue!"
>
> "Owl be back."

Harry Potter and the Prisoner of Azkaban (2004)

Voldemort follower Sirius Black (Gary Oldman) has escaped from prison and is coming after Harry.

> "Young wizard and Oldman."
>
> "Hermione watches her back."
>
> "Teenager learns to curse."
>
> "Potter faces Black magic."

GUESS THE MOVIE
"Edward Norton: Ire Man."

Harry Potter and the Goblet of Fire (2005)

Despite being too young, Harry is surprisingly picked to take part in the prestigious Triwizards Tournament. Harry develops a crush on a girl named Cho Chang.

> "Puberty's tougher than Voldemort."
>
> "Four wizards, a funeral."
>
> "Teacher has wandering pupil."
>
> "Potter vs. the Lakers."

Harry Potter and the Order of the Phoenix (2007)

Nobody believes Harry when he says Voldemort is back. Harry and his friends start a secret group called Dumbledore's Army. Harry and Cho start to develop feelings for each other. Sirius Black is murdered by his cousin Bellatrix Lastrange.

> "Bellatrix, Potter."
>
> "Sirius fades to Black."
>
> "Deathly Sirius."
>
> "Cho must go on."

Harry Potter and the Half-Blood Prince (2009)

A textbook Harry is using contains notes from the previous owner, the Half-Blood Prince, that allows Harry to excel in class. Harry falls in love with Ginny Weasley. Dumbledore is killed by Severus Snape.

> "The Snape's of Wrath."
>
> "Prince and the Potter."
>
> "Warning: wizard souled separately."
>
> "Dumbledead."

ANSWER

Jesus Cooks Me Breakfast (2007)

In this twenty-five-minute film, Jules gets a surprise visit from Jesus, who wants to make Jules breakfast and talk about God.

> "Turns water into . . . coffee."

> "Deviled eggs not eaten."

> "Father, Son, Holy Toast."

> "Heaven's plate."

The Lord of the Rings: The Fellowship of the Ring (2001)

A young hobbit named Frodo (Elijah Wood) begins an epic journey to Mordor to destroy a powerful ring. Peter Jackson directs the film version of the classic J. R. R. Tolkien book.

> "Hobbit gains elf-respect."

> "Jackson shoots J. R. R."

> "Child smuggling ring discovered."

> "Long, but hobbit forming."

The Lord of the Rings: The Two Towers (2002)

Frodo and Sam continue their journey toward Mordor. Pippin convinces the humanoid trees known as Ents to take part in the battle of Helm's Deep.

> "Gangs of New Orcs."

> "Trees lumber through forest."

> "The Ents go marching."

> "The Tree Amigos."

GUESS THE MOVIE "Tobey Maguire's webbed feat."

The Lord of the Rings: The Return of the King (2003)

Gollum (Andy Serkis) hunts down Sam and Frodo (Elijah Wood) as they get closer to destroying the ring. Aragorn (Viggo Mortensen) and the others take part in an epic battle of Middle-Earth.

> "Sequel with familiar ring."
>
> "Gollum loses precious, time."
>
> "One ring, 1,000 endings."
>
> "Elves left the building."
>
> "Sauron-arya."
>
> "Gollum gets the finger."
>
> "The Last Sam, awry."
>
> "Three. Ring. Serkis."
>
> "Sauron's lighthouse turned off."
>
> "Hard Hobbit to break."
>
> "The King and Eye."
>
> "Wood near the fireplace."

One Million Years B.C. (1966)

The most famous part of this caveman-and-dinosaur film is the iconic image of sexy bombshell Raquel Welch wearing an animal-skin bikini.

> "Raquel elicits group 'ug.'"
>
> "Bikini apparently early invention."
>
> "Cavewoman Welch invents erections."
>
> "Raquel Welch: Jurassic tart."

archer © istockphoto / fotko

ANSWER

Spider-Man (2002)

The Scorpion King (2002)

Dwayne (The Rock) Johnson plays Mathayus, a mercenary in ancient Egypt who rises to power to become the Scorpion King.

"Rock, pincers, papyrus."

"Rock Like an Egyptian."

"Rock and hard palace."

"The King of Rock."

The Stepford Wives (1975)

Why are all the wives in Stepford beautiful and loyal, and all love to clean and cook? The men of the town are secretly replacing their spouses with obedient robots.

"Husbands screw wives."

"Make my wife—please!"

"Chicks are really built."

"Wives require spousal battery."

Stranger than Fiction (2006)

Harold Crick (Will Farrell) is the only person who can hear an author (Emma Thompson) narrating his life. When the author reveals Harold is going to die, Harold must find her and convince her to change the ending of her story.

"Ferrell receives death sentence."

"Novel role for Ferrell."

"A plot against Will."

"Ferrell's a real character."

GUESS THE MOVIE "Beatty's Dick entices Madonna."

Twilight (2008)

Bella Swan moves to the small town of Forks and falls in love with Edward—a vampire who must curtail his blood-sucking instincts to be with her.

> "Teens have necking issues."
>
> "Civilized vampires use Forks."
>
> "Love without first bite."
>
> "Bella's a vamp eyer."

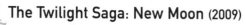

The Twilight Saga: New Moon (2009)

Edward and his family leave Forks. Heartbroken Bella finds comfort with childhood friend Jacob Black, who turns out to be a werewolf. Also starring Dakota Fanning.

> "Bella loves teen wolf."
>
> "Abandoned Swan discovers wolf."
>
> "Dakota Fanging."
>
> "Two-light."

The Twilight Saga: Eclipse (2010)

Bella and Edward are together again, but Bella must choose between the vampire and Jacob the werewolf. She also must decide if she wants to be immortal.

> "Trilight."
>
> "Suckers go for thirds."
>
> "Blood-crossed lovers wed."
>
> "Marriage marks Swan's song."

ANSWER

Dick Tracy (1990)

V for Vendetta (2005)

A knife-throwing vigilante (Hugo Weaving) known as V and styled after Guy Fawkes, terrorizes the powers-that-be in a dystopian Britain. Also starring Natalie Portman.

> "Knives and Fawkes."
>
> "Vicious vigilante vanquishes villains."
>
> "Guy Fawkes up London."
>
> "C'est la V."

Van Helsing (2004)

Famous vampire killer Van Helsing (Hugh Jackman—Wolverine from the *X-Men* movies) takes on Dracula, the Wolfman, and Frankenstein's monster.

> "X-man vs. ex-men."
>
> "Frankenstein wanted for battery."
>
> "Buff-guy the Vampire Slayer."
>
> "Count counterer counters Count."

GUESS THE MOVIE "Batty Bale battles Ledger."

The Wizard of Oz (1939)

A tornado sends Dorothy (Judy Garland) to the magical world of Oz. She travels down the Yellow Brick Road and meets the Scarecrow, Tin Man, and Cowardly Lion while trying to avoid the Wicked Witch of the West.

"Dandy lion."

"Lion, Witch, Wide Road."

"Dorothy drops in."

"Goodbye Yellow Brick Road."

"Gone with the Wind."

"Witch gets washed up."

"Nightmare on Em's Street."

"Dorothy is 'whirled' traveler."

"Witch has liquidation sale."

"Baum voyage."

"Yellow brick road trip."

"Wicked Witch's water weakness."

Xanadu (1980)

Olivia Newton-John plays a Muse who travels to Earth to inspire people to follow their dreams. The film, packed with disco music and roller-skating, was a critical flop.

"Heaven's Skate."

"Xana-don't."

"A Muse doesn't amuse."

"Xanadud."

ANSWER

The Dark Knight (2008)

This Chapter, Horror-bly Funny

➤ Horror ◄

28 Days Later . . . (2002)

A virus that turns people into raging zombies is accidentally released into the world. Twenty-eight days later, only a handful of human survivors are left and they must fight to stay alive.

> "The Livid Dead."
>
> "Rage against the vaccine."
>
> "Zombies solve traffic problem."
>
> "Ghouls of enragement."

GUESS THE MOVIE "Wife after death."

The Birds (1963)

Alfred Hitchcock directs this film about birds in a small coastal town that inexplicably start attacking humans.

>"Murder: fowl play suspected."
>
>"Psycrow."
>
>"Raven lunatics."
>
>"Unsettled bills cause anxiety."
>
>"Apocalypse Fowl."
>
>"The Hurt Flockers."
>
>"Cheep and nasty."
>
>"Death from a dove."
>
>"'Flocking hell!'"
>
>"Birds re-establish pecking order."
>
>"Coo d'etat."
>
>"A murder of crows."

The Blair Witch Project (1999)

This fake documentary follows three filmmakers who go into the woods to explore the legend of the evil Blair Witch. They become lost and realize they are being stalked.

>"Woman and map—disaster!"
>
>"America's Phoniest Home Video."
>
>"Hex, Lies, and Videotape."
>
>"S'not scary."

ANSWER

Corpse Bride (2005)

The Blob (1958)

A giant blob of red goo from outer space lands near a small town. It starts to grow as it consumes people and objects. The film stars Steve McQueen.

> "McQueen fights red menace."
>
> "Wild goo chase."
>
> "Jelly and I scream."
>
> "Goo: Bad and Ugly."

The Bride of Frankenstein (1935)

Dr. Frankenstein creates a wife (Elsa Lanchester) for his monster (Boris Karloff).

> "Dated monster movie."
>
> "My Big Eeeek Wedding."
>
> "Made for each other."
>
> "Stitch, suture, tie knot."

The Brides of Dracula (1960)

Baron Meinster, who is really Dracula, tries to seduce a young teacher and turn her into his vampire bride.

> "Brides have morning sickness."
>
> "Stake my wife, please!"
>
> "Down for the Count."
>
> "Polygamy sucks."

GUESS THE MOVIE "Scheider fears lone shark."

Carrie (1976)

A teenager with special powers (Sissy Spacek) is teased by classmates after she has her period in the locker-room shower. When a prank during the prom at the school's gym goes too far, she unleashes her revenge.

> "Menstrual psych hell."
>
> "Scarrie."
>
> "Gym Carrie's a riot."
>
> "Burning sensation follows period."

Children of the Corn (1984)

A couple stumbles into a small farming community where a young preacher has instructed the children to kill all the adults.

> "It shucked."
>
> "Little Crop of Horrors."
>
> "Children: farmed and dangerous."
>
> "Breed them and reap."

Christine (1983)

A high-school nerd buys and rebuilds a 1958 Plymouth Fury—a supernatural vehicle with a killer mind of its own.

> "Murder with auto-motive."
>
> "Plymouth should be repossessed."
>
> "Hell hath this Fury."
>
> "Mad, a gas car."

Cujo (1983)

After being bitten by a bat, a rabid dog terrorizes a mother (Dee Wallace) and son. Based on a Stephen King book.

> "Jaws on four paws."
>
> "Mad Dog and Gory."
>
> "Barking up wrong Dee."
>
> "Stephen King unleashes terror."

Dracula's Dog (1978)

Dracula's dog is accidentally unleashed from a tomb in Romania.

> "Tail from the Crypt."
>
> "Blood hound."
>
> "Bite worse than bark."
>
> "Spot of blood."

The Exorcist (1973)

Regan (Linda Blair) is a young girl who becomes possessed. She vomits and her heads spins around 360 degrees. Her mother and two priests try to save her.

> "Satan starts Regan revolution."
>
> "Possession 9/10ths of movie."
>
> "Room with a Spew."
>
> "Young Blair, head turner."

GUESS THE MOVIE "Huge Willy won't perform."

The Fly (1986)

A scientist (Jeff Goldblum) working on a teleporter accidentally transports himself and a fly. They are fused together and the scientist slowly starts turning into an insect.

> "Goldblum becomes a pest."
>
> "Goldblum needs SWAT team."
>
> "Scientist flies into rage."
>
> "Pretty fly white guy."

The Fog (1980)

A fog filled with turn-of-the century killer spirits engulfs a remote village and terrorizes the townspeople.

> "Mist ain't behavin'."
>
> "Murder: mist demeanor?"
>
> "Slay Misty for Me."
>
> "Killer's identity is unclear."

Frankenstein (1994)

Kenneth Branagh stars as Dr. Frankenstein and Robert De Niro is the Monster.

> "Doctor making a living."
>
> "Frankenstein: stark raving made."
>
> "Doctor sews wild oaf."
>
> "De Niro: made man."

Friday the 13th (1980)

Counselors at Camp Crystal Lake are stalked and killed. Starring Kevin Bacon. This is the first film in the horror franchise that features Jason, a hockey-mask-wearing killer.

> "Friday night. Saturday mourning."
>
> "Shrieky Friday."
>
> "Film initiates cinematic paraskavedekatriphobia."
>
> "Bacon gets sliced up."

The Hand (1981)

An artist (Michael Caine) loses his hand in an accident. The severed hand returns on its own and starts killing people.

> "Terror-wrist."
>
> "Hand solo."
>
> "Killer not easily fingered."
>
> "Hand on the run."

Hard Rock Zombies (1984)

A heavy metal band is murdered while on tour in a remote town, but they are brought back from the dead to help save a local woman.

> "Defunct band experiences revival."
>
> "The Hateful Dead."
>
> "Band stops performing live."
>
> "AC/DeCeased."

GUESS THE MOVIE "Fornicator hangs Dick out."

Hostel (2005)

Three backpackers travel to a hostel in Slovakia rumored to be filled with hot, promiscuous women. Instead of sex, they are kidnapped and sold to be tortured by rich businessmen.

> "Bed and deathfest."
>
> "Hostel: five-scar hotel."
>
> "Backpackers' inn trouble."
>
> "Run tourists, run!"

I Was a Teenage Werewolf (1957)

A doctor transforms a troubled teenager (Michael Landon) into a werewolf.

> "Michael Landon: beasty boy."
>
> "Boy who cried wolf."
>
> "Moon Landon."
>
> "American Werewolf in Landon."

Interview with the Vampire (1994)

A vampire named Lestat (Tom Cruise) tells his life story to a journalist. The film, based on an Anne Rice novel, also stars Brad Pitt and Kirsten Dunst.

> "From Dunst till Dawn."
>
> "Brad the Impaler."
>
> "Cruise's Lestat, somewhat Lecrap."
>
> "Pitt—Cruise's longtime companion."

ANSWER

Frost/Nixon (2008)

The Invisible Man (1933)

A scientist (Claude Rains) discovers a formula that makes him invisible but also slowly drives him insane.

> "Rains, Rains, go away."
>
> "Rains clears up."
>
> "Claude Rains is unwatchable."
>
> "Scarfface."

Jaws (1975)

Roy Scheider, Robert Shaw, and Richard Dreyfuss star in this film about a great white shark terrorizing the small island community of Amity.

> "Gone with the Fin."
>
> "Larger aquatic transportation required."
>
> "Gill against island."
>
> "Scheider fears lone shark."
>
> "Shaw Shark Redemption."
>
> "Music makes shark hungry."
>
> "Skinny-dipper becomes skinnier."
>
> "Eat ship and die."
>
> "Shooting barrel in fish."
>
> "Diet: fish and ships."
>
> "Amity's Vile Horror."
>
> "Missing license plate recovered."

GUESS THE MOVIE "Clothes encounters, 27th kind."

Killer Bees! (2002)

Nobody believes the town sheriff when he warns that deadly killer bees are headed toward the city.

> "Slaughterhouse Hive."
> "Natural Swarm Killers."
> "Movie generating killer buzz."
> "Attack of the Drones."

Killer Nun (1978)

Anita Ekberg plays a drug-addicted nun who wreaks havoc at a hospital.

> "Sister of no Mercy."
> "Sister: nun too kind."
> "Smother Teresa."
> "Bad habit."

Microwave Massacre (1983)

In this low-budget B-movie, a man kills his wife because of her poor cooking skills. He cooks her body in the family's large microwave and eats her.

> "Killing by unconvectional means."
> "Killer radiates evil."
> "Wife is smoking hot!"
> "The Ping and Die."

ANSWER

27 Dresses (2008)

Mime Massacre (2006)

In his funny (yet gory) short film available on YouTube, a man who hates mimes enters a room full of the silent, black-and-white performers and starts shooting, stabbing, and decapitating.

> "Silent *and* deadly."
>
> "All witnesses are mum."
>
> "Dead mimes. Happy ending."
>
> "Mime and Punishment."

Misery (1990)

A novelist (James Caan) involved in a car accident is rescued by a psychotic fan (Kathy Bates). She eventually breaks the writer's ankles with a sledgehammer to ensure he can't escape her home.

> "Foot loose."
>
> "Rabid fan de-feets Caan."
>
> "Another psycho Bates."
>
> "Bates worse than death."

Monsturd (2003)

In this B movie, a serial killer falls into a sewer full of chemicals. He is transformed into a half-human/half-shit killing machine.

> "Fecal madder."
>
> "Meet shit and die."
>
> "Public enemy number two."
>
> "Human waste wastes humans."

GUESS THE MOVIE "Emissions concern Clinton's VP."

The Mummy (1932)

Boris Karloff stars as a 3,700-year-old Egyptian mummy brought
back to life.

> "Karloff seeks new tailor."
>
> "America's first wrap star."
>
> "Stalk like an Egyptian."
>
> "Karloff: heir to eternity."

A Nightmare on Elm Street (2010)

In a remake of the classic 1984 horror film, a group of friends are
stalked in their dreams by killer Freddy Krueger (Jackie Earle Haley),
who wears a glove that has razors for fingers.

> "How Freddy Got Fingered."
>
> "Murder by Slumbers."
>
> "Insomniacs dread maniac."
>
> "Krueger's a sharp dresser."

The Omen (1976)

A U.S. diplomat (Gregory Peck) suspects his young child Damien
might be the son of Satan.

> "Damien is the demon."
>
> "Damien: cute little devil."
>
> "Peck has 666th sense."
>
> "Raise a 'little Hell.'"

ANSWER

An Inconvenient Truth (2006)

Poltergeist (1982)

Ghosts terrorize a family, kidnapping the young daughter to another dimension. The only way the parents can communicate with her is through the TV.

> "Captivated by TV snow."
>
> "Child watches absorbing television."
>
> "Must-flee TV."
>
> "TV's bad for daughter."

Psycho (1960)

This classic Alfred Hitchcock film is about Norman (Anthony Perkins), his mother, and the Bates Hotel. It features the famous scene where Janet Leigh is stabbed in the shower.

> "It's curtains for Leigh."
>
> "Unfortunate Leigh."
>
> "Norman is keeping Mum."
>
> "12, 11, 12 vacancies."

The Ring (2002)

A journalist (Naomi Watts) investigates the story of a mysterious videotape. Everyone who watches the tape supposedly dies seven days later.

> "Tape Fear."
>
> "VCR.I.P."
>
> "Vicious circle."
>
> "Video's late fee excessive."

GUESS THE MOVIE "Vaughn's Noel: no end."

Rosemary's Baby (1968)

Mia Farrow plays a woman who is carrying the unholy baby of a Satanic cult.

> "Housewife served deviled eggs."
>
> "Mamma Mia."
>
> "Rosemary faces inner demon."
>
> "Neighbors from Hell. Literally."

Santa's Slay (2005)

This film is about a killer Santa Claus.

> "On Slasher! On Hacker!"
>
> "Slashing through the snow."
>
> "Chestnuts roasting. *Open fire!!!*"
>
> "It's a Wonderful Knife."

Saw (2004)

Tobin Bell plays Jigsaw, a psychopath who places his victims in horrific quandaries to determine how far they would go to live. Cary Elwes plays a doctor trapped in a room who saws off his foot in order to escape.

> "Survival of de-footist."
>
> "Saw shank for redemption."
>
> "Cary Elwes—leg end."
>
> "Not saved by Bell."

Scream (1996)

A killer is stalking a group of teens according to the rules of horror movie deaths. The movie opens with the killer murdering Drew Barrymore. Also starring Neve Campbell.

"*Neve*r turn your back."

"Drew Nevermore."

"Drew's part short lived."

"Expressionist picture inspires trilogy."

The Shining (1980)

A writer (Jack Nicholson) and his family (including psychic son Danny) spend the winter taking care of the remote Overlook Hotel. Spirits drive Nicholson to try to kill his family.

"Jack should've 'overlooked' hotel."

"Psychic kid, also dyslexic."

"Jack'll nick his son."

"Jack of all tirades."

Silence of the Lambs (1991)

Clarice (Jodie Foster) seeks the help of Hannibal Lecter (Anthony Hopkins) to catch Buffalo Bill, a killer who is making a dress out of the skin of his victims.

"Cannibal shares chef tips."

"Kill to dress."

"Psycho gets under skin."

"Hannibal defaces state property."

GUESS THE MOVIE "Midget fights MiG jets."

The Sixth Sense (1999)

A child psychologist (*Die Hard* star Bruce Willis) tries to help out a boy (Haley Joel Osment) who sees dead people. The film is famous for a major twist at the end of the film.

> "Boy meets ghoul(s)."
>
> "Die Easy."
>
> "Small medium, large twist."
>
> "Tent isn't ghost proof."

Teeth (2007)

High-school student Dawn discovers a secret—she has teeth in her vagina, which she uses against overly aggressive males.

> "Dawn! That fucking hurts!"
>
> "Clit eats-wood."
>
> "Beaver likes gnawing wood."
>
> "Clam hides pearly whites."

Texas Chainsaw Massacre (1974)

Five friends are chased by a masked chainsaw-loving psycho known as Leatherface and his cannibalistic family.

> "Lumberjack the Ripper."
>
> "They came, they sawed."
>
> "Texas Tool and Die."
>
> "Leatherface plays Texas hole'm."

ANSWER

Top Gun (1986)

Vampire Circus (1972)

A circus run by vampires preys on local townspeople.

"These clowns suck."

"The Greatest Show Unearthed."

"Circus shuns tent stakes."

"Goes for the juggler."

GUESS THE MOVIE

"Gore's a warmmonger."

Italian–American Actors Pay Rent

→Mafia, Gangster, and Crime←

American Gangster (2007)

In the 1970s, Frank Lucas (Denzel Washington) becomes a popular drug kingpin in Harlem and Richie Roberts (Russell Crowe) is the detective trying to take him down.

> "Russell's Rich. Denzel's richer."
>
> "Crowe's feat—get Washington."
>
> "Washington is corrupt."
>
> "Frank: Harlem's robbin' hood."

Blood Vows: The Story of a Mafia Wife (1987)

In this made-for-TV movie, Melissa Gilbert plays a woman who marries an attorney, only to learn her new husband is the son of a powerful mobster.

> "Gilbert launders clothes, money?"
>
> "Hits and Mrs."
>
> "Sleeping with husband, fishes."
>
> "The Godfather-in-Law."

Bloody Mama (1970)

Ma Barker (Shelley Winters) leads her sadistic family on a crime rampage during the 1930s.

> "Weapon's of Ma's destruction."
>
> "Family that slays together . . ."
>
> "Barker family relatively evil."
>
> "Winters: cold-blooded killer."

Blow (2001)

Johnny Depp plays George Jung, one of the most powerful cocaine dealers in the United States during the 1970s. Penélope Cruz stars as Depp's wife.

> "Depp gets Blow job."
>
> "J. D. and coke."
>
> "Depp: 'I-deal' husband."
>
> "Invasion After Buddy Snitches."

Bonnie and Clyde (1967)

Warren Beatty and Faye Dunaway play the famous 1930s bank-robbing couple Bonnie Parker and Clyde Barrow, who die in a bloody shootout with law enforcement.

> "Parker gunned while parked."
>
> "Couple imitates Swiss cheese."
>
> "Bullets prevent Dunaway's getaway."
>
> "Runaway Dunaway adorin' Warren."

GUESS THE MOVIE "Stone's box 'orifice' hit."

Bugsy (1991)

Warren Beatty stars as Bugsy Siegel, a Jewish gangster who built the Flamingo Hotel and helped develop Las Vegas. Also starring Elliott Gould.

> "Conceiving Las Vegas."
>
> "One-man Kosher Nostra."
>
> "Mob deBugs Flamingo."
>
> "Vegas dreamer strikes Gould."

Bugsy Malone (1976)

All the gangsters in this family film, starring Jodie Foster and Scott Baio (Chachi from *Happy Days*), are played by children. The guns shoot cream, not bullets.

> "Child custardy battle."
>
> "Mafia in its infancy."
>
> "Jodie loves Chachi, underworld."
>
> "Mobsters just get desserts."

Carlito's Way (1993)

Carlito (Al Pacino) is an ex-con trying to go straight but his crooked lawyer (Sean Penn) pulls him back in.

> "Penn's no pal, Al."
>
> "Pacino's Penn won't right."
>
> "Brash Benny irks many."
>
> "Penn on diet: coke."

Casino (1995)

Ace (Robert De Niro) runs a Las Vegas casino on behalf of the mob. Things start to go downhill because of his drug-addict wife (Sharon Stone) and psychotic mob friend Nicky (Joe Pesci).

> "Pen mightier than neck."
>
> "Gangster's pair o' dice."
>
> "Of Dice and Men."
>
> "Coke-addicted Sharon stoned."

Collateral (2004)

A taxi driver (Jamie Foxx) is a hostage in his own cab when a hitman (Tom Cruise) forces him to drive around town as he takes out victims.

> "Meter, body count running."
>
> "Inevitable: death and taxis."
>
> "To Die Fare."
>
> "The Tominator."

The Departed (2006)

Matt Damon plays a cop who is secretly a Boston mafia mole while Leonardo DiCaprio is a cop who has infiltrated the mob. Both are trying to find out each other's identity.

> "Boston: rat-infested city."
>
> "Rat vs. mole."
>
> "Ratt Damon."
>
> "Damon has mob mentality."

GUESS THE MOVIE "Disfigured Merrick merits dignity."

Dog Day Afternoon (1975)

Sonny (*Carlito's Way* star Al Pacino) tries to steal from a bank to pay for his lover's sex change operation. But the robbery goes wrong and turns into a hostage situation.

> "Carlito's Gay."
>
> "Crime doesn't pay gay."
>
> "Financial 'trans' action."
>
> "Bank robbed for 'change.'"

Donnie Brasco (1997)

An FBI agent (Johnny Depp) infiltrates the mob and becomes so entrenched he loses touch with his family and starts sympathizing with his gangster friends.

> "The Depparted."
>
> "Donnie Depp."
>
> "Depp dupes diminutive don."
>
> "FuggetabouDepp."

Eastern Promises (2007)

The death of a pregnant teenager leads a midwife (Naomi Watts) into the seedy underworld of the Russian mafia. Viggo Mortensen (mob thug Nikolai) has a memorable full-frontal nude fight in a bathhouse.

> "Watts's midwife crisis."
>
> "Enjoy an in-Viggo-rating bath."
>
> "Viggo tries cock fighting."
>
> "Russian whoremongering: Ruskie business."

Fargo (1996)

Financially troubled Jerry (William H. Macy) hires two men to kidnap his wife so he can extort a large ransom from his father-in-law. One kidnapper (Steve Buscemi) is killed and his body is shredded in a wood chipper.

> "Parental Advisory: Chipper gore."
>
> "Chipper cop; chipped criminal."
>
> "Cop foils Macy's sale."
>
> "Kidnappers don't *go far.*"

Gangs of New York (2002)

In the Five Points area of 1863 New York City, an Irishman (Leonardo DiCaprio) seeks revenge on Bill "the Butcher" Cutting (Daniel Day-Lewis), who killed his father (Liam Neeson). Directed by Martin Scorsese.

> "Scorsese's bang-gang."
>
> "Five Points, yet pointless."
>
> "DiCaprio defeats defiant Day-Lewis."
>
> "Leonardo's fighting Irish."

GUESS THE MOVIE "Julia uncovers breasts, pollution."

The Godfather (1972)

Marlon Brando (Don Vito), James Caan (Sonny), and Robert Duvall (Tom Hagen) star in this Oscar-winning film about a young son (played by Al Pacino) taking control of the Corleone crime family. The mob sends a message by placing a horse's head in its owner's bed.

"Sonny doesn't buy happiness."

"Duvall's Advocate."

"Bed. Head."

"Sonny Corleone becomes holey."

"The Wrath of Caan."

"Corleone's greatest hits."

"For horseman, an apocalypse."

"Sleeping with fishes, horses."

"Sleeping with the equine."

"Sonny, bloody Sonny."

"Marlon Brando, hoarse whisperer."

"Sonny won't share."

The Godfather: Part II (1974)

The film tells parallel stories—young Vito Corleone's (Robert De Niro) rise to power in the 1910s and Michael Corleone's (Al Pacino) in the 1950s, who learns that his brother Fredo betrayed the family. Jewish mobster Hyman Roth gets whacked.

"Fredo should be afraido."

"Pacino wants casino."

"Old Hyman finally pierced."

"Sequel you can't refuse."

Erin Brockovich (2000)

The Godfather: Part III (1990)

Al Pacino tries to go legit but gets pulled back in. He gets involved with a corrupt Vatican official. The film features a performance from Sophia Coppola, the director's daughter, that was not well received.

> "I see dead papal."
>
> "Vatican promotes family values."
>
> "Sofia 'acts with fishes.'"
>
> "Offer you Vatican't refuse."

Goodfellas (1990)

This film tells the story of the rise and fall of gangster Henry Hill (Ray Liotta). Joe Pesci plays his psychotic mob friend who has the memorable "Funny, like a clown? I amuse you?" scene.

> "Pesci doesn't clown around."
>
> "Mole: Hill."
>
> "Pesci's House of Whacks."
>
> "Goodfellas commit bad felonies."

No Country for Old Men (2007)

Javier Bardem plays Anton Chigurh, a ruthless hitman whose favorite weapon is a cattle stun gun. He must track down a man who took $2 million during a drug deal that went bad.

> "Chigurh mortis."
>
> "Bardem: badass, bad hair."
>
> "The Anton Menace."
>
> "Bardem: stunning bad guy."

GUESS THE MOVIE "Dead people! I see!"

Ocean's Eleven (2001)

George Clooney, Brad Pitt, Matt Damon, and Julia Roberts star in
this heist film about Danny Ocean and his crew trying to rob three
Las Vegas casinos.

> "Pitt crew works fast."
>
> "Thieving Las Vegas."
>
> "Clooney's Ocean rather shallow."
>
> "The Money Pitt."

Ocean's Twelve (2004)

Terry Benedict (Andy Garcia) wants his money back, forcing Danny
Ocean (George Clooney) and friends to travel to Europe to try to
steal the famous Coronation Egg.

> "Cheater by the dozen."
>
> "Ocean, another drop in."
>
> "Trans-Atlantic Ocean."
>
> "Ironically, dozen steal egg."

Ocean's Thirteen (2007)

After a friend is double-crossed by ruthless businessman Willy Banks
(Al Pacino), Danny Ocean and his pals plan their revenge by trying
to bankrupt Banks's newest luxury casino.

> "Last Temptation of Heist."
>
> "Danny breaks the Bank."
>
> "Pacino crosses wrong Ocean."
>
> "Two too many Oceans."

ANSWER

The Sixth Sense (1999)

Once Upon a Time in America (1984)

This film follows the life of Jewish gangsters Noodles (Robert De Niro) and Max (James Woods) in New York from when they were children to their rise to power during Prohibition. Directed by Sergio Leone, who is most famous for his spaghetti Westerns.

> "Oy!-ganized crime."

> "Chosen people get made."

> "Spaghetti director, kosher Noodles."

> "Jew talkin' to me?"

Point Break (1991)

After a string of bank heists by crooks dressed as ex-presidents, FBI agent Johnny Utah (Keanu Reeves) attempts to infiltrate Bodhi's (Patrick Swayze) surfer gang, which may or may not be behind the robberies.

> "Surfs up! Hands up!"

> "To protect and surf."

> "Keanu surfs crime wave!"

> "Nixon *is* a crook."

Public Enemies (2009)

Johnny Depp stars as 1930s gangster John Dillinger, who is on the run from lawman Melvin Purvis (Christian Bale). The film is directed by Michael Mann.

> "Depp's Dillinger fights feds."

> "Gangster can't jump Bale."

> "Dillinger focus of Mann hunt."

> "Killer flees from Christian."

GUESS THE MOVIE "From acne to Arachne."

The Public Enemy (1931)

James Cagney plays a vicious hoodlum who rises to power in the Chicago underworld. The film is famous for a scene where Cagney rubs a grapefruit in the face of Mae Clarke.

> "Squeeze put on Mae."
>
> "Mae nominated: zest actress."
>
> "Clarke's face: fruit juicer."
>
> "James Cagney acts fruity."

Pulp Fiction (1994)

This Quentin Tarantino film stars Bruce Willis, Uma Thurman, John Travolta, and Samuel L. Jackson. Christopher Walken has a memorable scene about hiding a friend's watch up his ass while in a Vietnam POW camp.

> "Metric system renames burger."
>
> "John dies on john."
>
> "Foot massage causes disfigurement."
>
> "Travolta's career, Uma resuscitated."
>
> "Uma gets the point!!!"
>
> "Real shitty time travel."
>
> "Willis talkin' 'bout watch?"
>
> "Christopher Walken passes time."
>
> "Watch gets bum deal."
>
> "Willis saves Ving's ass."
>
> "Metric system amuses hitman."
>
> "Watch is crappy legacy."

ANSWER

Spider-Man (2002)

Reservoir Dogs (1992)

When a heist goes wrong, the thieves—who go by the names of colors (Mr. Orange, Mr. Pink, etc.)—discover one among them is an undercover cop. The film features a scene with Michael Madsen cutting off a cop's ear.

> "Orange paints floor red."
>
> "Madsen gives cop earful."
>
> "*Bang!* Au revoir dogs."
>
> "Crimes with Orange."

Road to Perdition (2002)

Tom Hanks plays a Depression-era gangster. When his son witnesses a murder, the mob wants the child dead. The pair go on the run. Jude Law plays a hitman sent to kill them.

> "Mobster Hanks robs banks."
>
> "Hitman runs from Law."
>
> "Father, son, holey gangsters."
>
> "Hanks fought, Law won."

Scarface (1983)

Al Pacino plays Cuban drug dealer Tony Montana, who comes to Florida and builds a powerful cocaine empire.

> "Manic Hispanic causes panic."
>
> "'Havana' Montana."
>
> "Florida defeat: Al, gore."
>
> "Little friend says hello."

GUESS THE MOVIE "The Cher Witch Project."

The St. Valentine's Day Massacre (1967)

The story behind Al Capone's gangland murder of seven mafia rivals on February 14, 1929.

> "Capone gets sweet revenge."
>
> "Mobsters aim for hearts."
>
> "Capone's pre-syphilitic VD."
>
> "Mobsters' heartless Valentine's massacre."

The Taking of Pelham 123 (2009)

Look Who's Talking star John Travolta leads a group of criminals who hijack a NYC subway. Denzel Washington plays the dispatcher who communicates with the hijackers. The film is a remake of a 1974 movie of the same name.

> "Pelham: one too many."
>
> "Travolta's evil loco motive."
>
> "Travolta: Look Who's Taking."
>
> "Subway, bloody subway."

Thelma and Louise (1991)

Louise (Susan Saradon) shoots a man who tries to rape Thelma (Geena Davis). With the police in pursuit, the female fugitives hit the road. The women ultimately escape—by driving their car off a cliff into a gorge.

> "Susan soar-on-down."
>
> "Women driver theories upheld."
>
> "Runaway women gorge themselves."
>
> "Girls hit rock bottom."

ANSWER

The Witches of Eastwick (1987)

The Untouchables (1987)

During Prohibition, federal agent Elliot Ness (Kevin Costner) and a Chicago beat cop (Sean Connery) go after mobster Al Capone (Robert De Niro).

> "Costner fights angry mob."

> "Costner's a fine Ness."

> "Law. Ness. Mobster."

> "Gangster faces taxing issue."

The Usual Suspects (1995)

SPOILER ALERT

A cop (Chazz Palminteri) interrogates crippled con man Verbal Kint (Kevin Spacey) and learns the story about a psychotic criminal named Keyser Soze.

> "Soze is all say-so."

> "Twisted foot plot twist."

> "Verbal Kint—Improv Tonight."

> "Chazz gets Verbal warning."

GUESS THE MOVIE "Dwayne Johnson: tough fairy."

These Are Un*four*gettable Films

↠ *Classics* ↞

12 Angry Men (1957)

During jury deliberations, Henry Fonda plays the lone man on a twelve-person jury who thinks a person accused of murder is innocent. Fonda gradually turns the opinions of the other jury members.

> "Fonda lacks conviction."
>
> "One relieved defendant."
>
> "Accused: 'Help me Fonda.'"
>
> "Accused overcomes 11/1 odds."

Abraham Lincoln (1930)

Director D. W. Griffith explores Abraham Lincoln's life, ranging from the president's early years to his assassination by John Wilkes Booth in Ford's Theatre.

> "Harrassed in Ford."
>
> "Fords fatal for Lincoln."
>
> "Inconvenient Booth causes gore."
>
> "President dis-Abe-led."

ANSWER

Tooth Fairy (2010)

The African Queen (1951)

Set in Africa during the First World War, a hard-drinking riverboat captain (Humphrey Bogart) is convinced by a missionary (Katharine Hepburn) to attack a German boat.

"Bogie gets Kate moist."

"Hepburn's My Ferry Lady."

"Rude dude ferries prude."

"Bogie, Hepburn take plunge."

All About Eve (1950)

A classic story about ambition and betrayal at a New York theater. Bette Davis plays veteran actress Margo. Anne Baxter is Eve, the young but manipulative up-and-comer.

"Understudy's underhanded ways."

"Bette battles backstage backstabber."

"Eve's all about evil."

"Two faces of Eve."

All the President's Men (1976)

The story of how two *Washington Post* reporters (played by Robert Redford and Dustin Hoffman) discover the truth behind Watergate and bring down President Nixon.

"Reporters' digging buries President."

"Dick Nixon's 'Post' mortem."

"Deep throat chokes Dick."

"When journalists had balls."

GUESS THE MOVIE
"Joan's superiors fire her."

Amadeus (1984)

Salieri (F. Murray Abraham) is the court composer in eighteenth-century Vienna who plots against young musical genius Wolfgang Amadeus Mozart.

> "Salieri orchestrates Mozart's murder."
>
> "Operatunists."
>
> "Mozart's 'mass' murderer."
>
> "Salieri has pianist envy."

American Graffiti (1973)

Star Wars creator George Lucas's coming-of-age film follows a group of teenagers who spend the night cruising around in cars. Starring Harrison Ford and Ron Howard.

> "Happy Days rough draft."
>
> "Ford races '55 Chevy."
>
> "Harrison prefers cruising solo."
>
> "Car Wars."

Apocalypse Now (1979)

During the Vietnam War, Martin Sheen travels down a river to kill renegade U.S. Colonel Kurtz (played by overweight *Godfather* star Marlon Brando).

> "Napalm makes military scents."
>
> "Brando: tribe's 'Odd-Father.'"
>
> "Soldiers fish for Marlon."
>
> "Kurtz needs to die(t)."

Ben-Hur (1959)

This biblical-era drama starring Charlton Heston won eleven Oscars and features a thrilling chariot horse race.

> "Speedway with real horsepower."
>
> "Hur Ben legend."
>
> "Jew overcomes race discrimination."
>
> "Nas-cart racing."

The Bridge on the River Kwai (1957)

During the Second World War, British and U.S. POWs build a railway bridge in Burma for their Japanese captors. But the Allies have plans to blow it up. Starring Alec Guinness.

> "Murdering an Orient Express."
>
> "Big bridge goes POW."
>
> "Londoner's bridge falling down."
>
> "Prisoners work for Guinness."

Butch Cassidy and the Sundance Kid (1969)

Butch Cassidy (Paul Newman) and the Sundance Kid (Robert Redford) are train robbers who flee to Bolivia to escape the law.

> "Newman kick-starts contest."
>
> "Robber Redford."
>
> "Redford's first Sundance festival."
>
> "Butch, Sundance's un-Bolivia-ble adventure."

GUESS THE MOVIE "Quint essential Coen flick."

Casablanca (1942)

Set in Africa at the start of the Second World War, American nightclub owner Rick (Humphrey Bogart) is surprised when Ilsa (Ingrid Bergman)—an old lover from Paris—walks into his bar.

> "Rick loses chick."
>
> "Bogart begins beautiful friendship."
>
> "France's capital fondly remembered."
>
> "Bergman picks Bogie-discards."
>
> "Paris makes Rick wet."
>
> "Bogey has a joint."
>
> "Sam gives repeat performance."
>
> "Usual suspects rounded up."
>
> "Tip off. Nice Berg'."
>
> "Bogie rediscovers Swede heart."
>
> "Here's looking at . . . quality."
>
> "Slut visits gin joint."

Chinatown (1974)

Jake Gittes (Jack Nicholson) is a private eye investigating a husband's affair. After getting his nose slashed by thugs, Jake discovers corruption related to the city's water department. John Huston plays Noah Cross.

> "Gittes's nose: director's cut."
>
> "Water scheme involving Noah."
>
> "Chinese. Water. Torture."
>
> "Gittes: dam nosey detective."

ANSWER

Raising Arizona (1987)

Citizen Kane (1941)

A reporter tries to find the meaning of Rosebud—the last, dying word of powerful newspaper tycoon Charles Foster Kane (Orson Welles).

"Kane remodels wife's room."

"Twist ending sleighs me."

"Kid's life goes downhill."

"Publisher has last word."

"Childhood memory fuels furnace."

"The Bad News Baron."

"Journalist, misled, misses sled."

"Xanadu, without the skates."

"Welles's performance re-Hearst."

"Drops dead. Sled."

"All sled and done."

"Kane's breakfast grows cold."

Cleopatra (1963)

This four-hour, big-budget epic is about Egyptian queen Cleopatra (Elizabeth Taylor) and her lover Marc Antony (Richard Burton).

"E.T. bones Rome."

"Liz Taylor barges in."

"Well-Taylored costume drama."

"My Pharaoh Lady."

GUESS THE MOVIE "Moore beats around Bush."

Cool Hand Luke (1967)

Luke (Paul Newman) plays a prisoner who refuses to conform. The film features a memorable scene where Luke attempts to eat fifty eggs in one hour, and the memorable line "What we got here is . . . failure to communicate."

> "Newman gets egged on."
>
> "Communication failure sinks Newman."
>
> "Little criminals. 'Randy' Newman."
>
> "Hard-boiled prison picture."

The Deer Hunter (1978)

Three friends (Robert De Niro, Christopher Walken, John Savage) discover the horrors of war in Vietnam. While in a POW camp, Vietcong guards force them to play Russian roulette.

> "Walken, De Niro click."
>
> "Russian roulette? Oh deer . . ."
>
> "Dead Man Walken."
>
> "Steelworker gets lead poisoning."

Deliverance (1972)

A canoe trip in the backcountry with four men turns into horror when one friend (Ned Beatty) is raped by rednecks. Also starring Burt Reynolds.

> "Dentist endures hillbilly proctology."
>
> "Warn Beatty!"
>
> "Beatty's vacation a bummer."
>
> "Whitewater shafting."

ANSWER

Fahrenheit 9/11 (2004)

Easy Rider (1969)

Captain America (Peter Fonda) and Billy (Dennis Hopper) ride motorcycles across the United States. They smoke pot, drop acid, meet a lawyer (Jack Nicholson), and try to discover the real America.

> "The Rollin' Stoned."
>
> "Grass, Hopper."
>
> "Hit the road, Jack."
>
> "Hopper on a chopper."

The Elephant Man (1980)

David Lynch directs the true story of John Merrick (John Hurt), a heavily disfigured man in nineteenth-century England who spends years as a sideshow freak before being saved by a doctor.

> "Hideous outside, Hurt inside."
>
> "Lynch mob chase freak."
>
> "A Merrick can dream."
>
> "Case of misshapen identity."

Gandhi (1982)

Ben Kingsley plays the Indian leader who used nonviolent techniques—such as fasting—to gain his country's independence from the British Empire.

> "The Fasting, The Furious."
>
> "Fastest man in India."
>
> "Starving for attention."
>
> "Hats off to Mahatma."

GUESS THE MOVIE "Thurman: The Lass Samurai."

The Gold Rush (1925)

A prospector (Charlie Chaplin) heads up to the Klondike to find gold and falls in love with a saloon girl (played by Georgia Hale). The film features memorable scenes of a starving Chaplin eating his boots, and making two forks with buns on the end dance on the table.

> "Laughs in a-bun-dance."
>
> "Chaplin strikes cinematic gold."
>
> "Tramp tries sole food."
>
> "Klondike cold. Georgia hot."

Gone with the Wind (1939)

Selfish Southern belle Scarlett O'Hara (Vivien Leigh) has a turbulent love affair with Rhett Butler (Clark Gable) during the American Civil War.

> "Rhett dumps selfish bitch."
>
> "Angry Scarlett sees Rhett."
>
> "Better Rhett than debt."
>
> "Slippery when Rhett."
>
> "Scarlett yearns, Atlanta burns."
>
> "The Scarlett Rhetter."
>
> "Belle without a cause."
>
> "Leigh serviced by Butler."
>
> "Damn not given, eventually."
>
> "Scarlett pregnant, Butler dunnit."
>
> "Rhett rings southern belle."
>
> "Scarlett teases wrong cock."

ANSWER

Kill Bill: Vol. 1 or 2 (2003/4)

The Graduate (1967)

Dustin Hoffman plays Benjamin, a young man seduced by his girlfriend's mother, Mrs. Robinson (Anne Bancroft).

"Anne's has-Ben role."

"Lust 'n' Hoffman."

"Likes mother. Likes daughter."

"Hoffman 'meats' the parent."

The Grapes of Wrath (1940)

During the depression, Oklahoma farmer Tom Joad (Henry Fonda) and his family flee the Dust Bowl and head to California.

"A Farewell to Farms."

"California or dust."

"Joads victims of home-icide."

"Joad trip."

The Great Escape (1963)

The true story of British and U.S. POWs who spend weeks secretly digging three tunnels. On the night of the escape, more than seventy prisoners get away. Starring Steve McQueen.

"POWs soil their pants."

"Steve McQueen gets cooler."

"Germans escape problems compounded."

"Great Escapism."

GUESS THE MOVIE "Moore's George W. Bash."

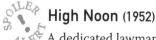

High Noon (1952)

A dedicated lawman (Gary Cooper) faces criminal Frank Miller and his gang alone after the townspeople refuse to help. Grace Kelly plays Cooper's new bride, who insists that he leave town to avoid the fight.

> "Noon? It's Miller time!"
>
> "Cooper: Grace or honor?"
>
> "12, angry men."
>
> "Everyone's chicken but Coop."

Hindenburg Disaster Newsreel Footage (1937)

A German passenger balloon goes up in flames as it tries to land in New Jersey. The famous 1937 disaster killed more than thirty people.

> "Full of hot error."
>
> "Ded Zeppelin."
>
> "Very hot air balloon."
>
> "Ironically, gas kills Nazis."

The Hunchback of Notre Dame (1939)

Charles Laughton plays deformed church bell ringer Quasimodo. When a beautiful gypsy is falsely accused of murder, Quasimodo tries to save her.

> "Slaved by the Bell."
>
> "Laughton plays dead ringer."
>
> "Laughton in striking performance."
>
> "Ringin' in the Seine."

ANSWER

Fahrenheit 9/11 (2004)

The Hustler (1961)

Small-time pool hustler, Fast Eddie Felson (*Cool Hand Luke* star Paul Newman), challenges legendary player Minnesota Fats (Jackie Gleason) to a big-stakes game.

> "Pool's full of sharks."
>
> "Cue Hand Luke."
>
> "The B&W of Money."
>
> "Rack and ruin."

Inherit the Wind (1960)

A science teacher is arrested for teaching Darwin's theory of evolution that humans evolved from monkeys. The film is based on the famous 1925 Scopes Monkey Trial.

> "Primate change: inconvenient truth."
>
> "Evolutionists swear on Bible!"
>
> "Monkeys 1. Bible 0."
>
> "Great create/primate debate."

It's a Wonderful Life (1946)

Classic Christmas film about an angel who shows a suicidal banker (Jimmy Stewart) what life would be like if he was never born. Lionel Barrymore plays grumpy Mr. Potter.

> "Potter defeated by magic."
>
> "Clarence wins wing clearance."
>
> "School dance ends swimmingly."
>
> "It's a wonderful film."

GUESS THE MOVIE

"Freeman, Nicholson: chemo sobbies."

King Kong (1933)

A giant ape is captured and taken to New York City. The beast escapes and climbs to the top of the Empire State Building. Fay Wray plays the woman King Kong falls in love with.

> "Kong gets stage fright."
> "***king huge gorilla."
> "Monkey falls for girl."
> "The original urban gorilla."

Kramer vs. Kramer (1979)

Dustin Hoffman and Meryl Streep play divorcing parents who fight for custody of their young son.

> "Divorce be with you."
> "Same name blame game."
> "I bet Kramer wins."
> "Battle of the Exes."

Lawrence of Arabia (1962)

British officer T. E. Lawrence (Peter O'Toole) organizes an Arab revolt against Turkey during World War I. Also starring Alec Guinness.

> "Turban Legend."
> "Warm Guinness—revolting!"
> "Brit deserts desert, dies."
> "Brit becomes oasis fan."

The Maltese Falcon (1941)

Sam Spade (Humphrey Bogart) gets mixed up with murder and shady characters who are all after one thing—a statue known as the Maltese Falcon.

> "Wants birdie, gets Bogie."
>
> "Spade seeks shifty statuette."
>
> "Spade digs up falcon."
>
> "Black Hawk Found."

Mary Poppins (1964)

Julie Andrews plays a magical nanny. This Disney film mixes music, live action, and animation and features the song "Supercalifragilisticexpialidocious!" Also starring Dick Van Dyke.

> "There's Some-sing About Mary."
>
> "Van Dyke's pseudo-cockney-unrealistic-especially-atrocious accent."
>
> "Diabetics: avoid this nanny."
>
> "Hootin' nanny."

Midnight Cowboy (1969)

Joe Buck (Jon Voight) is a naive male prostitute from Texas who comes to New York City and forms an unlikely partnership with a sleazy outcast named Ratso (Dustin Hoffman).

> "Tex and the City."
>
> "Buck in Bronx. Ho."
>
> "More bangs for Buck."
>
> "Ratso passes Buck stops."

GUESS THE MOVIE "Alcatraz broken into."

Miracle on 34th Street (1947)

Kris Kringle, a Macy's department store Santa, goes to court to prove he is the real Santa Claus and not an insane person. Starring Natalie Wood and Edmund Gwenn.

> "Santa's stamps of approval."
> "Believe Santa? Natalie would."
> "Santa goes postal."
> "Prosecution claims insanity Claus."

Moby Dick (1956)

Gregory Peck plays Ahab, the obsessed ship captain who will stop at nothing to find the huge white whale named Moby Dick.

> "Dick size *does* matter."
> "Ahab: 'Whale meet again . . .'"
> "Dick and sea men."
> "Whale feels Peckish . . ."

Old Yeller (1957)

Travis, a young boy from a poor family, befriends a stray dog named Old Yeller. The two bond but when the dog develops hydrophobia (rabies), Travis is forced to shoot his canine friend.

> "Hydrophobic liquidation draws waterworks."
> "Rabies cure = bullet."
> "Man kills best friend."
> "Pet Shot. Boys."

ANSWER

On the Waterfront (1954)

An ex-boxer (Marlon Brando) who could have been a contender works as a longshoreman on the docks and battles a corrupt union boss.

> "Brando feels pier pressure."
>
> "Non-contender gets contentious."
>
> "Wharfare."
>
> "Brando breaks union confederacy."

One Flew Over the Cuckoo's Nest (1975)

McMurphy (Jack Nicholson) is a convict sent to a mental ward who clashes with the wretched Nurse Ratched (Louise Fletcher), who is in charge of the ward. McMurphy inspires the patients to rebel against authority.

> "Irritable nurse loses patients."
>
> "Chief takes up plumbing."
>
> "Nut tries to bolt."
>
> "Psychiatrists don't know Jack."

Raging Bull (1980)

Robert De Niro plays boxer Jake La Motta, a violent man both inside and outside the ring. De Niro famously gained sixty pounds to play the older and fatter La Motta.

> "LaMotta: Aging Full."
>
> "Hello Motta, hello fatta."
>
> "Giving punches, then punchlines."
>
> "Middleweight gets heavier."

GUESS THE MOVIE

"Killer whale escapes imprisonment."

Rear Window (1954)

While confined to a wheelchair because of a broken leg, a bored photographer (Jimmy Stewart) spies on his neighbor (Raymond Burr) and suspects he committed a murder.

> "Stewart flashes his neighbor."
>
> "Stewart's neighbor's cold. Burr."
>
> "Hitchcock casts Stewart twice."
>
> "A peeper-view movie."

Rebel Without a Cause (1955)

James Dean plays a juvenile delinquent who is new in town. He fights with his parents and the school bullies. A game of chicken with stolen cars has tragic results. Also starring Natalie Wood.

> "Dean chokes on chicken."
>
> "Planetarium features shooting, stars."
>
> "Chicken kills."
>
> "'Dean' angst."

Reefer Madness (1936)

This anti-marijuana film is so over-the-top, it has become a cult classic. It tells a fictional tale about how smoking pot ruined the lives of a group of teens.

> "Eternal sunshine? Potless mind."
>
> "Weed: all about it."
>
> "Greatest Story Ever Rolled."
>
> "Fear the reefer."

ANSWER

Free Willy (1993)

Seven Brides for Seven Brothers (1954)

After Adam (Howard Keel) gets married, his six ill-mannered brothers decide they want to find wives as well.

"Seven brides, seven brooders."

"Super marry'o brothers."

"The Brothers Groom."

"The more, the marriers."

Singin' in the Rain (1952)

This musical's most famous scene has Gene Kelly dancing along a rain-soaked city street with his umbrella while singing the title song.

"The Wetting Singer."

"Kelly dances up storm."

"Splashdance."

"Drip, drop, tap, dance."

The Sound of Music (1965)

An ex-nun, Maria (Julie Andrews), is sent to the home of Baron Von Trapp (Christopher Plummer) to take care of his seven children. Soon their lives are in peril as the Nazis take over Austria.

"Mein Fair Lady."

"Plummer second to nun."

"Shut up hills!"

"Shut yer Trapps!"

GUESS THE MOVIE
"Denzel ELiminates Bible bashers."

A Streetcar Named Desire (1951)

An emotionally troubled Blanche DuBois (Vivien Leigh) moves in with her sister Stella and her brutish husband Stanley (Marlon Brando). Based on the play by Tennessee Williams.

> "Tennessee in Louisiana."
>
> "Tram, tramp both ridden."
>
> "Brando's performance: *Stella-r! Stella-r!*"
>
> "Strangers kind, relatives cruel."

Taxi Driver (1976)

Robert De Niro plays Travis Bickle, a NYC cabbie who becomes fed up with crime and sleaze and tries to help a twelve-year-old prostitute (Jodie Foster). Contains the classic line, "Are you talking to me?"

> "Bickle requests conversation clarification."
>
> "Death and taxis."
>
> "A Fare to Remember."
>
> "De Niro interrogates mirror repeatedly."

The Ten Commandments (1956)

Moses (Charlton Heston) receives the Ten Commandments from God, parts the Red Sea, and leads Hebrew slaves out of Egypt.

> "God dam!"
>
> "The Red Sea Strolls."
>
> "Bush talks, Heston listens."
>
> "Moses ready to humble!"
>
> "Apart tide."
>
> "Surf's up for Moses."
>
> "Ultimate judge gives 10."
>
> "Blessed Tide Story."
>
> "Rules set in stone."
>
> "Paramount releases prophet warning."
>
> "First ever perfect 10."
>
> "God prescribes two tablets."

To Kill a Mockingbird (1962)

Gregory Peck plays Atticus Finch, a Southern lawyer trying to defend an innocent black man in a racially divided Alabama town in the 1930s. Robert Duvall plays Boo Radley.

> "Guilty . . . of being black."
>
> "Duvall hardly says Boo."
>
> "Finch loses brief case."
>
> "Tried and Prejudice."

GUESS THE MOVIE "Skinny Keira seeks chest."

chariot © istockphoto / A-Digit

Movies with Four-Drawn Conclusions

⤞ *Animation* ⤝

Aladdin (1992)

Aladdin, a poor street rat, discovers a magic lamp with a genie (Robin Williams) inside. Aladdin uses his wishes to try to win the love of the beautiful Princess Jasmine.

> "Genie enables identity fraud."
> "Aladdin hits the bottle."
> "From rugs to riches."
> "Aladdin rubs, Robin comes."

Animal Farm (1954)

The classic George Orwell communist allegory sees barn animals lead a revolt against a human farmer. Once in charge, the pigs start changing the rules because not all animals are equal.

> "Inhuman portrayal of communism."
> "Boss hog."
> "Orwell's Notorious P.I.G."
> "Squealers ruin everything."

Bambi (1942)

After Bambi's mother is shot by hunters, the young deer learns to survive in the forest and makes friends with the other animals.

> "Disney makes a buck."
>
> "Mommy becomes trophy wife."
>
> "Running for deer life."
>
> "Deer today, gone tomorrow."

Beauty and the Beast (1991)

Belle is imprisoned in a castle by a hairy, mean beast, who needs somebody to fall in love with him in order to break a curse.

> "Chewbacca gets laid."
>
> "Saved by the Belle."
>
> "Belle gets Stockholm Syndrome."
>
> "Annoying teapot spouts advice."

Bee Movie (2007)

Jerry Seinfeld plays a bee who takes humans to court after he learns they are taking and eating honey. Renée Zellweger plays Jerry's love interest.

> "Hive talkin'."
>
> "Men beehiving badly."
>
> "Show me the honey!"
>
> "Renée is Jerry's honey."

GUESS THE MOVIE "Matt Dillon fingers suspect."

Bolt (2008)

Bolt (John Travolta) plays a superhero dog on a TV show who doesn't realize his superpowers aren't real. Bolt travels across the country (with a hamster in a plastic bubble) to reunite with his owner, Penny.

> "Pup, pup, and away."
>
> "Ballsy hamster crosses America."
>
> "John Travolta's pup fiction."
>
> "A Penny saved."

A Bug's Life (1998)

After grasshoppers threaten his colony, Flik heads out to find warrior ants to defend them. The film is very similar to another cartoon ant film that came out in 1998, *Antz*.

> "War and Remember*antz*."
>
> "Combat-ants."
>
> "Anty hero."
>
> "Flik flick."

Cars (2006)

This Pixar film features an arrogant racecar, Lightning McQueen, who is sentenced by a judge to spend time in tiny Radiator Springs.

> "McQueen discovers his routes."
>
> "Car 'toon."
>
> "Braking news! Lightning's missing!"
>
> "Art your engines."

CInderella (1950)

This classic Disney tale is about evil stepsisters, a Fairy Godmother, and a glass slipper.

> "Housekeeper swept off feet."
> "Shoe must go on!"
> "Nice mice aid maid."
> "Shoe size determines royalty."

Corpse Bride (2005)

In this Tim Burton film, a man (Johnny Depp) practicing his wedding vows in the forest accidentally marries Emily, a beautiful woman who happens to be dead.

> "Depp gets a boner."
> "Re-animatrimony."
> "For better, for hearse."
> "The bride is late . . ."

The Dish Ran Away with the Spoon (1933)

In this short film, dishes and utensils dance and fight with food.

> "Everything's out of sink."
> "That's all, forks!"
> "The Plate Escape."
> "A fleeing saucer."

GUESS THE MOVIE "Hitler's days are numbered."

Dumbo (1941)

A baby elephant in the circus is teased because of its enormous ears.
With the support of a friendly mouse, Dumbo learns to fly.

> "Elephant is drawing, flies."
>
> "Dumbo jet."
>
> "Earplane."
>
> "Elephant flaps. Audience claps."

Fantasia (1940)

This Disney cartoon features various shorts set to classical music.
The Sorcerer's Apprentice short features Mickey Mouse battling
brooms carrying buckets of water.

> "The Apprentice: 'You're fired.'"
>
> "Mickey sweeps to stardom."
>
> "Waltz Disney."
>
> "LSDisney."

Finding Nemo (2003)

In this Pixar movie, an overprotective clownfish journeys across
the ocean to find his son, who has been captured and placed in an
aquarium in a dentist's office.

> "Rebellious son gets tanked."
>
> "Display of fish guts."
>
> "Missing *poisson*."
>
> "The Bait Escape."

Happy Feet (2006)

An emperor penguin in the Antarctic named Mumble cannot find a mate because he can't sing. He soon discovers he has another talent—tap-dancing.

> "Shiverdance."
>
> "Frigid air's Fred Astaires."
>
> "Polar ice tap."
>
> "Emperor's New Groove."

Horton Hears a Who! (2008)

Horton (*Ace Ventura* star Jim Carrey) discovers a microscopic town of Whos living on a speck of dust. He must protect the speck because none of the other animals believe the Whos exist.

> "Ace Ventura: Speck Protective."
>
> "Who group surprisingly quiet."
>
> "Look, Whos talking."
>
> "Who's there?"

Ice Age (2002)

A woolly mammoth (Ray Romano), saber-toothed tiger (Denis Leary), and a sloth find a human baby and must return it to the tribe. Scrat, the acorn-loving squirrel, is the film's scene stealer.

> "Romano Leary of humans."
>
> "Three mammals, a baby."
>
> "Much Ado About Nuttin'."
>
> "Squirrel's nuts freeze."

GUESS THE MOVIE
"Brando: dock-u-drama."

The Incredibles (2004)

A family of secret superheroes must unite to defeat the evil mastermind Syndrome. Holly Hunter provides the voice of the mother/Elastigirl. Brad Bird writes and directs.

> "Family downs Syndrome."
> "It's Bird's plain supermen."
> "Elastigirl remains A cup?"
> "Wife stretched to limits."

The Jungle Book (1967)

Mowgli is a boy raised by wolves. When the jungle animals (including Baloo the bear) learn man-eating tiger Shere Khan has returned, they try to send Mowgli to a human village for safety.

> "Wrath of Shere Khan."
> "Black panther fights adversity."
> "Rhythm and Baloo."
> "The Sound of Baloo-sic."

Kung Fu Panda (2008)

A fat, uncoordinated panda (Jack Black) is surprisingly picked to become a great kung fu master.

> "Pow! Smack! Bam . . . boo."
> "Fists of Furry."
> "Beats, Shoots, and Leaves."
> "Panda is Black, white."

The Lion King (1994)

King Mufasa is killed by his evil brother Scar, who has tricked prince Simba into believing he was responsible for his father's death. Years later, Simba is asked to return and take his rightful place as king.

> "Father of the Pride."
> "Today's gnus: Mufasa trampled."
> "Lion, cheatin', and stealin'."
> "The lion weeps tonight."

The Little Mermaid (1989)

Mermaid Ariel trades her voice to evil sea witch Ursula for a pair of legs so she can go on land. Ariel has three days to make Prince Eric, a human, fall in love with her.

> "Mermaid lands a prince."
> "Princess: Little re-tail value."
> "Flock of sea-gals."
> "Decisions: Wife or sushi?"

Madagascar (2005)

A group of New York City zoo animals (voiced by *Zoolander* star Ben Stiller and Chris Rock) escape and find that life in the wild is not like life in the zoo.

> "Penguins steal ship, show."
> "Chris Rock possibly white."
> "Stiller a zoo lander."
> "The Crate Escape."

GUESS THE MOVIE "Wahlberg's biggest part yet!"

The Man with the Smallest Penis in Existence and the Electron Microscope Technician Who Loved Him (2003)

In this eight-minute animated short (which can be seen on YouTube), Chester Gaylord goes to the doctor and a beautiful technician tries to help him with his 'small problem.'

> "Condom minimum."
>
> "Hung like a horsefly."
>
> "Microscoprick."
>
> "Itsy bitsy teenie weenie."

Monsters, Inc. (2001)

Hairy blue monster Sulley (John Goodman) and the giant-eye Mike (*When Harry Met Sally* star Billy Crystal) are experts at scaring kids. But chaos ensues when a cute girl named Boo enters their monster world.

> "When Hairy Met Sulley."
>
> "Cutie and the Beast."
>
> "Goodman makes good monster."
>
> "Kid makes eye scream."

Mulan (1998)

A young woman in ancient China disguises herself as a man and joins the army to fight the invading Huns.

> "Ori-Yentl."
>
> "Mulan Ruse."
>
> "Cross-dresser saves China."
>
> "Chinatoon."

ANSWER
Boogie Nights (1997)

The Nightmare Before Christmas (1993)

Jack Skellington of Halloween Town discovers Christmas Town. Jack loves the idea of Christmas so much that he arranges Santa's abduction and delivers presents to children in a coffin-like sleigh. Sally is secretly in love with Jack.

"The Worst Noel."

"Hell of a Christmas."

"Jack: rebel without Claus."

"Sally's a material girl."

One Hundred and One Dalmatians (1961)

A family of Dalmatians battles evil Cruella De Vil, who is collecting the adorable black-and-white spotted canines to turn them into a Dalmatian-skin coat.

"See spots run."

"One big yappy family."

"Animation 101."

"Cruella guilty of littering."

Peter Pan (1953)

Peter Pan is about a boy who never grew up. Peter visits three children and takes them on a magical flight to Neverland where they run into the evil Captain Hook.

"Hook stirs flying Pan."

"Boys harassed in Neverland."

"Constant-teen."

"Typical male never matures."

GUESS THE MOVIE "Remains *in* the Day."

Pinocchio (1940)

A wooden puppet, whose nose grows every time he tells a lie, dreams of becoming a real boy.

> "Walk, the Pine."
>
> "Lies = facial Viagra."
>
> "Knotty boy."
>
> "Everyone nose he's lying."

The Pirates Who Don't Do Anything: A Veggietales Movie (2008)

Larry the Cucumber and two friends are magically sent back in time to the 1700s and embark on a pirate adventure. All the characters in this movie are fruits and vegetables.

> "Patch-eyed peas."
>
> "Pirates of Carob Bean."
>
> "They don't 'produce.'"
>
> "Berried treasure?"

The Polar Express (2004)

A boy who doesn't believe in Santa Claus boards a magical train that takes him to the North Pole. Tom Hanks plays five different roles in this 3D film, including the train conductor.

> "Thomas the Hanks Engine."
>
> "Yule express Christmas doubts."
>
> "Claus encounters, 3D kind."
>
> "Santa's train of thought."

Ratatouille (2007)

Remy the rat loves to cook and becomes a chef in a Paris restaurant by guiding a clumsy garbage boy from beneath his hat. The two form an unlikely partnership.

> "Remy stirs up trouble."
>
> "Of Mice and Menus."
>
> "Rat makes tasty meal."
>
> "Cook discovers hat cuisine."

The Real Story of Humpty Dumpty (1990)

Glenda Jackson and Huey Lewis provide the voices in this tale about the famous egg that sat on a wall and had a great fall.

> "The dangers of crack."
>
> "Humpty can't contain himself."
>
> "Humpty invents base jumping."
>
> "Star has breakthrough performance."

Shark Tale (2004)

When the son of a shark mob boss is found dead, little fish Oscar (*Fresh Prince of Bel-Air* star Will Smith) takes the credit. But the mob boss (*Goodfellas* star Robert De Niro) wants revenge in this underwater mafia film.

> "Goodfilets."
>
> "Gill Smith."
>
> "Fresh Prince. No air."
>
> "Smith's Oscar-swimming performance."

GUESS THE MOVIE "Stripper: just add water."

Shrek (2001)

To save his swamp, grumpy ogre Shrek (Mike Myers) and an annoying donkey (Eddie Murphy) must rescue Princess Fiona (Cameron Diaz).

> "Grim fairy tale."
>
> "Forest Grump."
>
> "Murphy talks out ass."
>
> "Ogre achiever."

Shrek 2 (2004)

Shrek, now married to Princess Fiona, spends time with his in-laws and must deal with sword-wielding cat Puss In Boots, an evil Fairy Godmother and her son, Prince Charming.

> "Cute pussy, great ass!"
>
> "Shreks after marriage."
>
> "Puss comes to shove."
>
> "Boots made for stalking."

Shrek the Third (2007)

When Princess Fiona's frog father King Harold dies, Shrek tries to convince a distant heir—nerdy, awkward Artie (*NSYNC singer Justin Timberlake)—to assume the throne. Shrek also becomes a daddy.

> "Heir of the frog."
>
> "Star Shrek's next generation."
>
> "Third Shrek? Ohhh grrr."
>
> "Shrek, Artie not *NSYNC."

ANSWER

Flashdance (1983)

The Simpsons Movie (2007)

TV's most famous yellow family comes to the big screen. After Homer spills a silo full of pig poop into a lake, the government places a large dome over Springfield.

> "Eat my feature lengths."
>
> "Why, Caramba?"
>
> "More doh for Groening."
>
> "Had me at yellow."

Sleeping Beauty (1959)

After being cursed by an evil sorceress, Princess Aurora falls into a deep sleep when she pricks her finger on a spinning-wheel needle. A kiss from a prince awakens Sleeping Beauty.

> "Kiss undoes prick."
>
> "Asleep at the wheel."
>
> "Spinning makes princess faint."
>
> "Regally Blonde."

GUESS THE MOVIE "Rehearsals?! Is that it?"

Snow White and the Seven Dwarfs (1937)

When a magic mirror tells the wicked queen she is no longer the fairest maiden in the land, Snow White flees into the forest and takes refuge with the seven dwarfs. The dwarfs work as miners.

"Bad choice, upon reflection."

"Hymen has seven dents."

"Seven miners dig, princess."

"Six adjectives, one occupation."

"Powerful McIntosh—sleep mode."

"Witch makes Snow fall."

"Dwarves play miner roles."

"No-longer-unaccompanied miners."

"Prince comes, girl asleep."

"Princess dwarfed by cast."

"Minor miners mind maiden."

"Mine is short-staffed."

Spirited Away (2001)

In this Oscar-winning Japanese film, a young girl and her parents take a wrong turn and end up in a mysterious town. Along the way, her parents are turned into pigs.

"Hogs. Wash."

"Rewis Caroru."

"Parents swindled, become swine."

"Alice-san in wonderland."

ANSWER

The Tortoise and the Hare (1935)

The classic tale of the fast, cocky rabbit who races a slow tortoise. The rabbit is so far ahead, he stops to take a nap and the tortoise ends up winning the race.

> "Pride lets hare down."
>
> "Tortoise's hare-racing adventure."
>
> "Fast and the Furriest."
>
> "Unexpected hare loss."

Toy Story (1995)

Toy cowboy Woody (Tom Hanks) becomes jealous when little boy, Andy, gets a new, favorite toy—action figure Buzz Lightyear (Tim Allen).

> "Woody/Allen engages child."
>
> "Toys with my emotions."
>
> "Cartoon with moving conclusion."
>
> "Boy gets first Woody."

Toy Story 2 (1999)

Woody is taken by a greedy toy collector. Buzz Lightyear and his toy friends head out into the real world to rescue Woody.

> "Toy tale recall."
>
> "Conflicting loyalties—Woody's torn."
>
> "Two infinity and beyond."
>
> "Stinky Pete jerks woody."

GUESS THE MOVIE "Patrick Swayze: Bar Wars."

Up (2009)

Carl Fredricksen (Ed Asner) is a grumpy old man who ties thousands of balloons to his home, lifting it into the air and taking him on a journey to South America. He doesn't realize there is a stowaway— an eight-year-old boy.

"Inflation causes housing crisis."

"Asner in suspended animation."

"Old man raises child."

"Asner's Up-lifting adventure."

"House flies."

"Home and away."

"Asner gets it up!"

"Fredricksen gets carried away."

"Dreams balloon into reality."

"First international domestic flight."

"Drifter snatches boy scout."

"Retiree has mobile home."

WALL-E (2008)

This Pixar film is about the last remaining trash-collecting robot alone on Earth. Alone that is, until another robot comes to the planet looking for signs of life.

"WALL-E follows BOOT-E call."

"Loner stalks vegetation evaluator."

"Short film gets compacter."

"Waste lot, want 'bot."

balloons © Adams Media

ANSWER

(1989) Road House

Yellow Submarine (1968)

The Beatles (John, Paul, George, and Ringo) travel to Pepperland to take on the Blue Meanies.

> "Yellowship of the Ringo."

> "Starr vehicle."

> "Beatlemarinia."

> "Pstarring psubmarine, psongs, psychedelia."

GUESS THE MOVIE
"Carrey's thought-revoking film."

Scenes, but Not Heard

→→ *Silent Movies* ←←

Watch these movies online at
www.fourwordbook.com/theater.

Nowadays, there's a truly mind-boggling selection of films freely available on the Internet. Don't worry—they're not all bad, and in some cases you won't even feel dirty inside after watching them. In fact, if you know where to look, there's a veritable bounty of historical films to be found online.

This chapter is dedicated to such films. Sure, you're unlikely to find any of these at the local multiplex and most have a running time of less than two minutes. (*The Handshake*, for example, is just three seconds long, meaning it'll actually take you less time to watch than to read the reviews.) But we just felt these reviews were too good to pass up.

For your convenience (and to show we're not just making this stuff up), all the films in this chapter can be watched right now and for free directly from our website at *www.fourwordbook.com/theater.*

With all that said, welcome to the Four Word Film Review theater. Take a seat, relax, and enjoy the films. Oh, and try not to spill your drink—we only had this carpet cleaned last week.

Alice in Wonderland (1903)

The classic Lewis Carroll story sees Alice (played by May Clark) follow a rabbit down a tunnel and enter a magical world. Time: eight minutes.

> "Alice has tunnel vision."
>
> "Girl explores magical hole."
>
> "Lewis (Carroll) and Clark."
>
> "Alice takes bad trip."

Annie Oakley (1894)

Legendary sharpshooter Annie Oakley shows off her shooting skills by blasting glass balls and other objects. Time: twenty-five seconds.

> "Shooting missus never misses."
>
> "Annie gets her gun."
>
> "Shooting star."
>
> "Oakley: a glass act."

The Barbershop (1894)

In this film by the Edison Manufacturing Company, a man gets a shave in a barbershop while two customers wait and chat. Time: forty-four seconds.

> "Edison displays cutting wit."
>
> "Clippin' it old skool."
>
> "Lather seen, blather unheard."
>
> "Edison's first director's cut."

GUESS THE MOVIE "Ferrell's 'write' to live."

The Birth of a Nation (1915)

This film about the Civil War is a cinematic landmark and was the highest-grossing movie ever at the time. The film is very controversial today because it portrays the KKK as heroes. Time: three hours.

> "Kauses Kuite the Kontroversy."
>
> "KKK gets silent treatment."
>
> "KKKlassic."
>
> "KKK OK? No way!"

Blacksmith Scene (1893)

Three blacksmiths bang on iron while drinking beer. Time: thirty seconds.

> "Swig while iron's hot."
>
> "Hot bangers with ale."
>
> "Hammering, getting hammered."
>
> "Men forge a relationship."

The Boxing Cats (Prof. Welton's) (1894)

Two cats wearing boxing gloves punch each other while in a mini boxing ring. Time: twenty-five seconds.

"Ali cats."

"Litter boxers."

"Pussy gets a pounding."

"No scratching below belt."

"A real catfight."

"Limited to nine rounds."

"Left-right upper cat."

"Puss in bouts."

"MeOW!"

"Southpaws?"

"Flail of Two Kitties."

"Cat smack fever."

The Boys Think They Have One on Foxy Grandpa, but He Fools Them (1902)

Two boys hand Foxy Grandpa a banjo and laugh. But Foxy Grandpa plays like a professional and performs amazing dance moves. The two boys look on in amazement. Time: one minute, twenty-five seconds.

"Grandpa strings boys along."

"Grandpa outfoxes boys."

"Senior's superior strutting skills."

"Foxy fingers boys' instrument."

GUESS THE MOVIE "Frost hammers stiff Dick."

Cattle Driven to Slaughter (1897)

A herd of cattle go through the stockyards on the way to a slaughterhouse. Time: thirty seconds.

> "An udder blood bath."
>
> "There Will Beef Blood."
>
> "Apocalypse Cow."
>
> "No more bull shit."

A Chess Dispute (1903)

Two men in a restaurant get into a fight over a game of chess. Time: one minute.

> "Chess pains."
>
> "Black/white knight fight."
>
> "Tempers go unchecked."
>
> "Chess players, no mates."

The Cock Fight (1894)

Two roosters fight each other. Time: forty seconds.

> "Fighting cocks aren't chicken."
>
> "Cocks, a duel do."
>
> "Poultry in commotion."
>
> "Referee sees two fowls."

cat © Neubau Welt

ANSWER

A Morning Bath (1896)

A mother washes her young baby boy. As the suds and water splash all over the baby, he begins to cry. Time: forty seconds.

> "Movie's star has tantrum."
>
> "Child actor washed up."
>
> "Bath's plot wishy-washy."
>
> "Tub, scrub, and suds."

A Corner in Wheat (1909)

A rich businessman tries to corner the world wheat market. The price of bread skyrockets, driving the grain producers toward poverty. Time: fourteen minutes.

> "Wheat makes bread."
>
> "Wheat smell of success."
>
> "Barley, watchable."
>
> "Haulin' oats."

The Dancing Skeleton (1897)

A skeleton dances as various bones fall off the body and magically reattach themselves. Time: forty-five seconds.

> "Humerus film about dancing."
>
> "The Graceful Dead."
>
> "R.I.P. the light fantastic."
>
> "Dancer's a little stiff."

GUESS THE MOVIE "Newman's slap stick comedy."

Demolishing and Building Up the Star Theatre (1901)

Using time-lapse photography, this film shows a theater in New York completely dismantled and torn down. Time: one minute, forty-five seconds.

> "Star: stage and screen."
>
> "Theatrical remake."
>
> "Star destroyers."
>
> "A falling star."

Dog Factory (1904)

A butcher runs a machine called the Patent Dog Transformator. Dogs are dropped into the machine and transformed into sausage. The sausage is put in the machine and live dogs are made. Time: four minutes.

> "Dogs 'meat' weird change."
>
> "Ruff day at factory."
>
> "Bark, 'wurst . . . then bite?"
>
> "Boxers dropped, wieners appear."

Driving Cows to Pasture (1903)

Cowboys round up and move a herd of cattle. Time: one minute.

> "Raising the steaks."
>
> "Wrangler management."
>
> "Steaks on a plain."
>
> "Silent moovie."

Edison Kinetoscopic Record of a Sneeze (1894)

Edison Manufacturing Company employee Fred Ott takes a pinch of snuff up his nose and sneezes. Time: four seconds.

> "Lights, camera, ah-choo!"
>
> "Edison makes snuff film."
>
> "Fred Ott blows snot."
>
> "Original Hollywood boogeyman."

GUESS THE MOVIE
"Actually, speeding bullet faster."

The Execution of Mary Stuart (1895)

This film re-enacts the beheading of Mary, Queen of Scots for conspiring to assassinate Queen Elizabeth I. Time: eighteen seconds.

"Mary receives trial, separation."

"Stuart whittle(d)."

"Queen given the ax."

"Elizabeth severs diplomatic relations."

"Mary: original dead head."

"Queen's last live appearance."

"Mary, head of state."

"Elizabeth orders bloody Mary."

"Mary Choppins."

"There's Something Off Mary."

"Royal pain in neck."

"Mary displays acting chops."

Fun in a Bakery Shop (1902)

A baker plays with dough, sculpts it into funny faces, and throws it at another baker. Time: one minute, thirty-eight seconds.

"Waiting for 'good dough.'"

"Roll on floor laughing."

"Crumby humor."

"Fun where yeast expected."

axe © Neubau Welt

ANSWER

The Gay Shoe Clerk (1903)

Two women enter a store. The salesman places a shoe on one of the woman and then starts kissing her. The other woman then starts hitting the salesman with an umbrella. Time: one minute, thirty seconds.

> "Bawdy and sole."
>
> "Happy, feet."
>
> "Early foot fetishist film."
>
> "Gay clerk not homosexual."

Glenroy Brothers (Comic Boxing) (1894)

One boxer fights with a traditional boxing style while the other fighter flips and jumps around. Time: twenty seconds.

> "Brotherly gloves."
>
> "Comics deliver punch lines."
>
> "Glenroy's jab well done."
>
> "Brothers miss each other."

The Great Train Robbery (1903)

Director Edwin Porter's cinematic classic sees Broncho Billy and his gang of bandits stop a train and steal from the passengers. The film ends with a shootout between the cops and the robbers. Time: ten minutes, twenty-five seconds.

> "Baddie Broncho Billy bagged."
>
> "Train gets held up."
>
> "Train. Porter."
>
> "Police 'track' down robbers."

GUESS THE MOVIE "Cage against the machines."

The Handshake (1892)

This extremely short Thomas Edison film features two people shaking hands. Time: three seconds.

> "Edison's camera hand-ling: shake-y."
>
> "A gripping tale."
>
> "Hand it to Edison."
>
> "Cinema's first hand job."

How a French Nobleman Got a Wife Through the *New York Herald* Personal Columns (1904)

A French nobleman places an ad announcing any woman who wants to get married should meet him the next day at 10 a.m. A dozen women show up and chase him around the countryside. Time: eleven minutes.

> "Personal leads to physical."
>
> "French nobleman's engaging comedy."
>
> "Run for your wife."
>
> "Franco-American relationship heralded."

Jack and the Beanstalk (1902)

Jack trades the family cow for some magic beans. The next morning, the beans have turned into a giant beanstalk. Jack climbs and finds himself in the home of a giant. Time: ten minutes.

> "Stalk footage."
>
> "Green movement takes off."
>
> "End justifies the beans."
>
> "The vine intervention."

ANSWER

Gone in Sixty Seconds (2000)

Japanese Acrobats (1904)

One Japanese acrobat lies on the floor and uses his feet to flip and turn the other acrobat. Time: one minute, forty-seven seconds.

"Turning Japanese."

"Revolutionary Japanese cinema."

"Storyline has many twists."

"Japanese actors' early 'roll.'"

Jeffries and Ruhlin Sparring contest at San Francisco, Cal., November 15, 1901 (1901)

The highlights of the boxing match between James Jeffries and Gus Ruhlin. Time: two minutes, thirty seconds.

"Silent but Jeffries."

"Film pulls no punches."

"Beats of San Francisco."

"Ruhlin clash."

Life of an American Fireman (1903)

Firefighters rush into a burning building and save a mother and her toddler. Time: six minutes.

"Burn, baby burn. Inferno."

"Burning desire—save child."

"Mother has smoking problem."

"To blazes with America!"

GUESS THE MOVIE

"Marriage is the 'Pitts.'"

Love in a Hammock (1901)

A man and woman kiss and hug while in a hammock, unaware of the two mischievous boys behind them. Time: one minute.

> "Both lovers well hung."
>
> "Swingers."
>
> "Cot in the act."
>
> "Aroused by knotty lines."

Nanook of the North (1922)

Considered cinema's first full-length feature documentary, this film follows one year in the life of an Eskimo named Nanook as he hunts and plays in the Canadian Arctic. Time: one hour, eighteen minutes.

> "Nanook's a cool guy."
>
> "Snow place like home."
>
> "ColdPlay in Canada."
>
> "Nanook goes with floe."

New York City 'Ghetto' Fish Market (1903)

People explore the stalls of a turn-of-the-century fish market in New York City. Time: two minutes.

> "Good show, old chum."
>
> "Suffers from stalled narrative."
>
> "Sell-fish New Yorkers."
>
> "Something fishy about NYC."

ANSWER

Mr. & Mrs. Smith (2005)

Nosferatu (1922)

This German film features actor Max Schreck playing one of the scariest vampires in cinematic history. Audiences were terrified by his pointed ears and claw-like hands. Time: one hour, twenty-four minutes.

> "Schreck nailed the sucker."
>
> "Nosferatu: silent but deadly."
>
> "Vlad Max."
>
> "Schreck's a bloody ogre."

Panorama of Eiffel Tower (1900)

Men and women walk around the base of the Eiffel Tower. The camera pans up and down to show the height and beauty of the Paris landmark. Time: one minute, thirty seconds.

> "The Eye-full Tower."
>
> "Towering achievement in cinematography."
>
> "Landmark in French cinema."
>
> "Erection's entire height profiled."

Pillow Fight (1897)

Four teenage girls jump out of their beds and start to have a pillow fight. The pillows break open and feathers fly everywhere. Time: twenty-seven seconds.

> "Featherweight fight."
>
> "Young girls get 'down'."
>
> "The Bedding Slingers."
>
> "Four play in bedroom."

GUESS THE MOVIE "Marky Marksman"

Soldiers Washing Dishes (1898)

Soldiers line up to wash and dry their dishes. Time: thirty-six seconds.

> "Company, dish missed!"
>
> "Death before dish honor."
>
> "They dried for freedom!"
>
> "Silent grime fighters."

Trapeze Disrobing Act (1901)

A female trapeze artist starts taking off her clothes as two men from the balcony cheer her on. Time: two minutes, twenty seconds.

> "Discarded clothes hanger."
>
> "Strip bar."
>
> "Stripper found on-line."
>
> "Disrobing woman a swinger."

A Trip to the Moon (1902)

In this classic French film, a group of scientists board a rocket and visit the moon and discover hostile inhabitants. The film utilizes innovative special effects, including the famous shot of the rocket landing in the moon's eye. Time: ten minutes, thirty seconds.

> "No CG Eye used."
>
> "Apollo 1902."
>
> "Paris, we've a problem."
>
> "First moon mission faked!"

What Happened on Twenty-third Street, New York City (1901)

People walk along a New York City street. At the end of the film, a woman steps on a sidewalk grate and a gust of wind blows her skirt up. Time: one minute, twenty seconds.

> "Lifted skirts . . . very NYC!!!"

> "Woman receives blow job!"

> "Woman's passing wind problem."

> "Lady skirts around traffic."

The Wonderful Wizard of Oz (1910)

This silent, short black-and-white version of Frank L. Baum's novel was made almost three decades before Judy Garland's more famous *Oz* movie. Time: thirteen minutes.

> "Follow gray brick road."

> "Soundless over the rainbow."

> "Shortest Oz trip ever."

> "Toto-ly awesome silent movie."

The Wright Brothers (1908)

Orville and Wilbur Wright demonstrate their new flying machine while in France in 1908. Time: one minute, thirty seconds.

> "The Wright Stuff."

> "To air is human."

> "Wrights are soar winners."

> "Wright's future looking up."

GUESS THE MOVIE "Lord of the Sing."

And Now the Credits . . .

→→ A List of Contributors ←←

The Four Word Film Reviews website now boasts more than 10,000 extremely succinct Roger Ebert–wannabes. While many of these are from Britain, America, Canada, and Australia, regular contributors also reside as far away as Singapore, Croatia, Israel, Thailand, Turkey, and Poland. Basically, we're a bit like highly niche (and, frankly, somewhat rubbish) superheroes—wherever there is a movie showing, wherever there is pun injustice to be done, there we will be . . . furiously summing up the darned movie in four words or less.

We couldn't possibly hope to fit the work of each and every one of these hardy folks in one book, but we tried . . . boy, did we try. The names that follow are what can best be described as a ridiculously long list of people who have written reviews that are in this book. A list that includes a lawyer from Los Angeles, a copyeditor at one of Canada's largest newspapers in Toronto, a computer programmer from Melbourne, an actress from London (who has performed alongside Woody Allen, Warren Beatty, and Barbra Streisand), plus the usual bunch of Internet loners, shut-ins, and psychopaths.

They are brilliant, inspired, and generous, deserving all the credit for making this book such enormous fun. Some people are identified by a combination of their real names, FWFR username, hometown, and a four-word message. Others preferred to remain anonymous, choosing to be credited only by their username for reasons we've been legally advised not to ask.

Srinivas (aahaa, muahaha) G.; India; "Four words should do."

Adam (Adam Grilli) Grilli; Great Dunmow, Essex, UK; "4 words? Perfectly adequate."

Airbolt

Al Swearengen

Ali (Ali) Arikan; Istanbul, Turkey; "Turk that!"

Andrew (Andrew) Lydon; Galway, Ireland

Alex (Animal Mutha) Muth; Porthcawl, Bridgend, South Wales; "Who woulda thunk it."

Toby (AussieCanuck) Malone; Toronto and Perth; "Reviewing Four Australia, Canada."

Beth (BaftaBabe) Porter; USA and UK; "fwfr—my only addiction!"

Bavvy

Benjamin (Beanmimo) Moore; Dalkey, Co. Dublin, Ireland; "Exclude me in here!!"

benj clews; London, England; "Much shorter in person."

Ben (bennyr81) Rose; Manchester, England

Bernie (Bernie) Keating

Martin (bife) McGregor; Newbury/Singapore; "Kai's stolen my xBox."

Douglas (BiggerBoat) Bebb; London, England; "Bigger, faster, stronger . . . drunker."

Brian (Boydegg) Boyd; Llantwit Major, Wales; "Check out Grammarman Comic."

Donovan (Brass Johnson) Johnson; Columbus, OH; "Life, Movies, Pursuit, Happiness!"

Brent (brentrn) Thompson; New London, PA; "Clews' reviews offer clues."

Brody (B-ROD) Kenny; Lexington, KY; "The shorter the better."

Colin (c dot) Mancer; Toronto, Canada; "Enjoy! Here's three more."

Chris (calmer) Ifekwunigwe; Los Angeles, CA; "Sensibly seeking self-stimulation."

GUESS THE MOVIE "Kill Hitler: Mission impossible."

Curt (Canklefetish) Bizovi; Newark, DE; "Fwiffering keeps Cankle content."

Catuli

Charles (chazbo) Harding; Denver, CO; "Looking back, pressing fourword."

David (Cheddar's Finest) B. Macdonald; Cheddar, Somerset, UK; "Believe in Blue Birds!"

Cheese_Ed; Colby, 'Whizconsin', USA; "Molds reel cheesy editorials."

Davida (ChocolateLady) Chazan; Jerusalem, Israel; "Chocolatey Delicious and F(WFR)amous!"

Chris (Chris C) Coolbear; Bucklesham, England; "Four words, never backwards."

Gary (clay) W. Bowers; Phoenix, AZ; "GREAT Succinctness Training! Thanks!!"

Dave (Conan the Westy) Westaway; Ballarat, Australia; "Free film fun. Fanks!!"

Joy (Corduroy Pillow) Yokoyama; Kingston, Canada; "It's a punderful life."

Richard (CrackerJack) Hoffman; Butler, PA; "Flicks site picks rights!"

Malcolm (damalc) C. Knox; Louisville, KY; "DON'T steal this book."

Dan (danimal) Meyer; Orlando, FL; "Four thumbs up!"

Dante (Dante) A. Bacani; Chicago, IL; "Grateful to be included!"

Dave (davedavedave) Cappuccitti; Newmarket, ON

Dominic (demonic) Brewer; London, England.

dgbenner

djw1973; "Show me the money!"

Douglas (Dovaj) Orlyk; Bloomingdale, IL; "Honored to be included."

A. (Downtown) David Brown; Boston, MA; "Four me, for you."

drossolalia

durianfan

E.L.F.; Brightlingsea, Essex, UK; Small, but perfectly formed!"

Alex (el guapo) Rose, Manchester, England

elchico

Mike (Eminence Front) Ford; Brick, NJ; "Sun shines. People forget."

Andrew (EvilAndy) Scott Wells; Jefferson City, MO; "Laughing at verbosity's expense."

Falken

Fresno

Scott (Gentleman Ghost) Harrison; Aptos, CA; "Brevity: soul of wit."

Guy (GHcool) Handelman; Los Angeles, CA; "Acknowledgment is empowerment."

gobsmacker

Rick (Grumpy) Harris; Wellington

Heather

George (hustleboy007) Litman; Marietta, OH; "Thank you, Benj Clews!"

Jeffrey (JanglerNPL) Harris; Nashville, TN

Joe (Joe Blevins) Blevins; Arlington Heights, IL; "Swell idea this, Benj!"

Anthony (Josh the cat) Cadle, East Yorkshire, England; "Shortened reviews, heightened enjoyment."

Justin credible

Ken (Ken) Kie; Chicago-ish, IL; "I'm in a book!"

knockmesi10y

Dave (Koli) Collier; Newport; "Striving lackadaisically for perfection."

Tom (kolo) Colley; Motown, USA; "kolo salutes Benj's book."

Kruegerbait

LadyMeerkat

Noel (lamahasuas) O'Hora; Bristol, UK; "I give up. Almost."

Larry (Larry) Stallings; Orlando, FL; "Fourtunate to be included."

Larry (Larry B) Brown; Waterloo, Canada; "Next stop: five words!"

Jim (lemmycaution) Grace; Toronto, Canada; "Marilyn's fourbearance gracefully acknowledged."

Lindsay (Lindsa) Mutch; Wellington, New Zealand; "Film: Seeing is disbelieving."

Lindsey (Lindsey K) Kalenborn

Gene (Little Old Lady from Dubuque) Perry; Dubuque, IA; "Decidedly NOT a 'Lady'!"

LPH

Paul (mampers) Mampilly; Basildon, UK; "The FWFR abides man."

Chris (mandodgingdebris) Brown; Nashua, NH

GUESS THE MOVIE "Jock fears athletic supporter."

marina

Mark B

Mark (Markandlain) Westaway; Brisbane, Australia; "fwfr forever."

Matt ([matt]) Roach; London, England; "To awesome four words."

Melissa (MelissaS) Smith; Brunswick, Australia; "Thankyou my moviegoer friends."

John (MguyX) W. Mustafa; Los Angeles, CA; "I'm loving every minute."

MisterBadIdea

Nicholas (MM0rkeleb) Rupprecht; Gurnee, Illinois, USA; "God bless the FWFR!"

Emily (Montgomery) Desmond; Huntington Woods, MI; "Thanks for including me."

Eric (Mr Savoir Faire) Yesbick; Leesburg, GA; "I'm published! Hi Mom!"

noc

Paul (noncentz) Coyne; Los Angeles, CA; "Master of fourin' language."

Eoin (numbersix_99) O'Faolain; Dublin, Ireland; "I'd like to thank . . ."

Owen (Obie) Burn; Newport, South Wales; "Four: Bex, Molly, Evan."

Paddy (Paddy C) Corry; Dublin, Ireland; "The answer is 42."

Paul Bennison; Lickey End, Worcestershire, UK

Pope George Ringo

Adam (punz) Spellicy; Melbourne, Australia; "Abridged too far?"

Sarah (Puzzgal) Dickey; St. Louis, MO

quartet4

rabid kazook

randall; New York, NY; "Wisecrackers fill book? Unreal!"

Real-life Lisa

RedKate; New York, NY

Tom (redPen) Pender; Macon, GA; "FWFR = fabulous film fun!"

RockGolf; Canada

Rohan (Rocat) Jayasekera; Toronto, Canada; "Next: FWBR for books."

Ken (rockfsh) Kuniyuki; Honolulu, HI; "Madison, not yet four."

Ian (Rovark) Elliott; Eltham/ London, UK; "Life's lived four-words."

ANSWER

The Fan (1996)

Sean (Seán) McGrath; New Zealand; "I like four play."

shoon

Brian (silly) Reeves; Texas;

David (Sludge) Wolfberg; Los Angeles, CA; "Dear Hollywood: I apologize."

Dustin (Smeghead) Hedin; Taylorsville, UT; "Thanks Benj! Cool website!"

Tom (soda) de Kryger; Holland; "Seems funnier on paper."

Sam (SoS) Goodwin; Reading, England; "FWFR Amusement Park. Punland."

spoon

Karen (Stalean) Dawes Colley; Sterling Heights, MI; "Thanks for the memories."

stroll

Suzie (suzie) Philippot; Calgary, Canada; "She lives fo(u)r words."

David (The Prof) Hannah; Vancouver, Canada; "A book? Great idea!"

Mario (thefoxboy) Lanza; Melbourne, Australia; "Four your eyes only."

Brandon (TitanPa) Hower; Williamsport, PA; "Striving four better words."

Victoria (Tori) Keen; Fort Worth, TX; "I don't get it."

tortoise; Sussex, UK; "Don't applaud, throw money."

Bryan (Turrell) Turriff; Little Rock, AR; "Thanks four the fun!"

Warzonkey

Weeble-head Boy

Scott (Wheelz) McLean; Naperville, IL; "Grateful four the recognition!"

Jeff (Whippersnapper) Goldberg; London, England; "Coulda been a somebody . . ."

Liz (Wildheartlivie) Patrick; Indiana; "Watching hard, writing harder."

Stan (Yelnats) Morris; Sydenham, Ontario, Canada; "Better late than never."

Tony (Yenser) Johnson; Stockport; "Fanks. Wonderful For Relaxation."

Michael (Yukon) Onesi; Kingston, Canada; "Publishing: I'm not Clew-less."

Ian (zulu) Bendelow

GUESS THE MOVIE "As the Crowe lies."

Index